D0122054

race
& class
on campus

race
& class
on campus

conversations with Ricardo's daughter

JAY M. ROCHLIN

The University of Arizona Press   Tucson

The University of Arizona Press
© 1997 Jay M. Rochlin
All rights reserved

∞ This book is printed on acid-free, archival-quality paper.
Manufactured in the United States of America

02 01 00 99 98 97   6 5 4 3 2 1

Library of Congress Cataloging-in-Publication Data
Rochlin, Jay.
Race and class on campus : conversations with Ricardo's daughter /
Jay M. Rochlin.
p. cm.
Includes bibliographical references and index.
ISBN 0-8165-1670-7 (cloth : acid-free). — ISBN 0-8165-1671-5 (pbk. :
acid-free)
1. Minority college students—Arizona—Tucson—Case studies.
2. University of Arizona—Alumni and alumnae—Interviews.
3. Hispanic American college students—Arizona—Tucson—History.
4. Afro-American college students—Arizona—Tucson—History.
5. Arizona—Tucson—Race relations—Case studies. I. Title.
LC3732.A6R63   1997
378.1'9829—dc21   96-45817
CIP

British Library Cataloguing-in-Publication Data
A catalogue record for this book is available from the British Library.

Publication of this book is made possible in part by the proceeds of a
permanent endowment created with the assistance of a Challenge Grant
from the National Endowment for the Humanities, a federal agency.

In many ways this book is about pioneers, people who dared to explore new territory. I dedicate it to two women who demonstrated for me the strength it takes to walk the uncharted course.

To me, it was just how Grandma talked. But my dad, aunts, and uncles tell me that few sentences came out of her mouth without a fairly random mix of Spanish, English, and Yiddish.

Fleeing persecution and seeking a better life, Annie Rochlin left Russia as a teenager. She entered the United States in New York, met Jake, crossed Canada, and re-entered this country at Vancouver. I've never seen immigration papers. She, Jake, and their three children arrived in Nogales, Arizona, in August 1917. One of those children was my dad. He was five months old. In Nogales, she and her family learned Spanish, then English, opened a small store, and made a home for themselves and their family.

Claire Rochlin grew up in Brooklyn and loved New York City. A child of Jewish immigrants, she thrived on the lights, crowds, Macy's, Broadway, and Fifth Avenue. Her life took a different turn when she met and married a soldier from Arizona. In 1946, Claire moved to Nogales to begin life with Abe. She took to the community and it took to her. She raised her family, gave more than she took, and left those who knew her richer, always ready to smile, and more willing to love.

< Contents

The one thing that each of us knows is that the way we
have been going until now is not the way. Now come, let
us join hands and look for the way together.

—Rabbi Hayyim of Zans

I met Fred Acosta when he was president of a group called Hispanic
Alumni. He told me about coming back to the University of Arizona
after fighting in the Korean War and facing blatant racism in many
of his classes. I remember telling myself that I should record Fred's
stories.

At the same time, while working at the university's Alumni
Association, I noticed how rare it was to see Hispanics or blacks at
university reunions. But some attended. At the fiftieth reunion for
the class of 1940, I met Mildred Hudson McKee. She told me about
one class in which the professor made her and the two other black
students sit in the back of the room, separated from white students by
a row of seats. But, she added, during the second half of the semester,
black students got to sit in the front, with the white students in the
back.

Three years later, I heard Laura Banks, at her fiftieth reunion,
tell how she almost didn't graduate because she couldn't pass the
swimming component of her physical education class. The reason:
black girls weren't allowed in the university's swimming pool.

Fred Acosta died early and unexpectedly. I was sad for his
family and many friends. But I also mourned the loss of his stories,
his part of the narrative of the Mexican American experience at the
university. Fred's passion for education, his empathy for minorities,
and his untimely death were among the reasons I decided to collect
the stories of others who succeeded in the pursuit of education.

This book is about twenty-nine Mexican American and sixteen
African American men and women who attended the University of
Arizona and "made it." I hope the description of their lives and personal educational experiences over eight decades will help readers
gain a greater appreciation for the issues faced daily by scholars,
administrators, faculty, and more importantly, by millions of individuals and their families for whom the question of college is vital,
the sacrifices real.

While minority status can be claimed by Hispanics, African
Americans, Asian Americans, Native Americans, women, gays,

lesbians, religious minorities, people with disabilities, and older groups, just to name a few, I restricted this inquiry to individuals who self-identify as Mexican American or African American. They represent the University of Arizona's largest and most visible groups of people who have been subject to racial or ethnic discrimination or abuse nationally, or as identified by John Ogbu, represent, other than Native Americans, America's most visible and victimized castelike minorities. I chose not to include Native Americans in this study because I believe that population is diverse and it is misguided to define Native Americans as a homogeneous group.

The university opened in 1891 on a barren plot of desert a mile east of Tucson. Old Main, the first structure, is a two-story brick building, framed by mesquite trees and cactus, on the far west side of campus, a quaint reminder of education's early entry into the life of the Old West. Looking east from Old Main's second-story veranda, a visitor sees the university's signature feature, a wide, grassy mall lined with palm trees where students from around the country work on their Arizona tans. The mall is flanked by large classroom buildings and a student union.

Today, Arizona is a 35,000-student research university surrounded on all sides by a growing city. The campus is home to a medical college, a law school, and world-class departments of astronomy, space science, optics, and anthropology. But it's still trying to do a good job teaching freshmen and sophomores, and like most of the nation's universities, it is struggling to deal with issues of race and class.

The situation in Tucson, and at the university, is unusual. The city has more than 600,000 residents, most of whom are Anglo Americans who were born somewhere else. The same is true of faculty members and senior administrators. Few claim southwestern roots.

People like Fred Acosta noticed these things. He described the alienation the Mexican Americans he grew up with felt toward the university. He looked around his neighborhood and saw friends, or children of friends, who were just as smart and hardworking as the university students. Why were those who attempted a college education such exceptions? He wondered why large numbers of Chicanos weren't continuing their educations by taking advantage of this excellent school less than two miles from their homes.

When Fred came to college in the 1950s, he didn't know terms like "class theory," "stratification," or "institutional racism." He simply thought the "folks at the university didn't like Mexicans." Even so, he graduated in 1960 and spent the rest of his life giving others the hope that they, too, could achieve a college education.

But the racial climate on many American campuses remains a barrier to those hopes. Even though it has been more than forty years since *Brown v. Board of Education* and more than thirty years since the Civil Rights Act of 1964, the fundamental problem of racism remains unsolved.[1]

We read reports describing racially motivated beatings or vandalism aimed at individuals, often involving Nazi or Ku Klux Klan symbols. Other incidents are more complex and deadly. On August 20, 1990, a University of Arizona policeman was shot and killed after responding to a report of trouble at a fraternity party. A black teen, a local high school student, was arrested. The kid admitted carrying a firearm and shooting it into the air. But he said he was provoked when frat boys called him "nigger." Police reports later revealed that the fatal bullet came from a fellow policeman's pistol. Even so, the teen was charged with murder and served time in jail.

And in 1996, Mexican American students held candlelight vigils outside a university fraternity house to call attention to their claim that a fellow student had been called a "spic" by a member of that house.

Even for those minority students who never suffer the indignities of overt racial harassment, their experience is often difficult and sometimes impossible due to more subtle barriers based on race, ethnicity, or class.[2] Measures designed to help—affirmative action, race-based admissions criteria, and scholarships—are under fire from legislators, regents, and trustees in many states, notably California.

Over the past thirty years, universities have made a variety of efforts to recruit and retain minority students. Yet it remains a harsh fact that a disproportionately small number of African American and Mexican American students complete college degrees. That record of futility convinced researchers of the need to ask new questions and use new tools to find out why.

Some writers suggest the problem of race in America might never be solved, only better understood, and perhaps better coped with. They call their point of view "critical race theory." As I researched and wrote this book, I used the narrative techniques and outlooks of various critical race theorists.

These writers, mainly academics of color, are disturbed at what they view as retrenchment from the civil rights gains of the 1960s. According to Richard Delgado, one of the field's leaders, they see themselves as tokens, their scholarship marginalized, their numbers few and stagnant.[3]

Because traditional scholarship failed to address issues of concern to these and other writers, they began to experiment with new forms. Derrick Bell, in his groundbreaking *And We Are Not Saved: The Elusive Quest for Racial Justice,* used dreams, stories, dialogue, and science fiction to illustrate the many points he hoped to make. Others turned to personal histories, poetry, and parables to demonstrate important messages about race in America.

Most critical race theorists reject the idea that "color blindness" will lead to either justice or equality. They say we must look at issues in a "race conscious" way or forever continue to see white culture as superior.[4]

Critical race theorists have also examined the classroom.[5] They claim objectification, subjectification, and alienation are problems faced by students of color and urge the use of personal perspectives in the classroom, arguing that failure to do so only supports the dominant perspective. Delgado believes people of color are different from their white counterparts because minorities experience racism virtually every day, while whites rarely experience or even notice acts of subtle or overt racism.

With that theoretical grounding, and the certain knowledge that many of the university's early students wouldn't be around to tell their stories in another ten years, I began interviewing for this book. The stories I heard were powerful and contained much to teach and inspire.

To help frame the stories about university life as a minority person, I created Gabriela Valenzuela. She is loosely based on the daughter of a friend of mine from high school. For the most part, though, she is a product of my imagination, a means of sharing the stories, experiences, and ideas that emerged from my interviews.

Gabriela is a seventeen-year-old high-school senior struggling to decide whether to pursue a college degree. Through a series of conversations, she and I explore aspects of the minority experience in a university environment through the eyes of the people who've been there. My hope is that Gabriela can embody thousands of American young people for whom the pursuit of higher education is a difficult, but possible, dream.

Other than Gabriela and her mom and dad, all names, places, and events are written as they were told to me, with some minor alteration of language for flow and clarity.

The men and women I interviewed for this book generally entered "helping" professions. Many became educators. They spend discretionary time speaking to young people about the value of education and personal responsibility. Many serve on commissions and committees, speaking out for education and opportunity, and encouraging others to do the same. They were willing to share their stories and allow me to use their real names because they believed young people might benefit from reading about their experiences.

My fear that these stories, if left unrecorded, could be lost was well-founded. Even before I completed the first draft, Elgie Batteau, Malachi Andrews, and Mildred Hudson McKee, three of the people I interviewed, died.

Elgie Mike Batteau entered the University of Arizona and graduated ten years later. Many of southern Arizona's older generation of black leaders, including several in this book, credit their success to Elgie. She taught many of them at Dunbar, Tucson's segregated elementary school. Malachi Andrews was the university's first Olympian. He graduated in 1955 and became a professor of art in California. Mildred McKee graduated in 1940. She had a three-decade-long career as a teacher and counselor in the Stockton, California, school system. Her children went on to become successful professionals.

When I think about the lives of the four generations of former students I interviewed, I think of words like persistence, drive, ambition, and discipline. But even more, I am struck by their enduring optimism in the face of grinding racism, discrimination, bigotry, and class oppression. I tried to use their words to impart some of that optimism and hope to Gabriela and other young people considering college.

One of my greatest difficulties in writing this book was coming to terms with the continued existence of racism and its effects on individual students, and the need to pursue fairness and opportunity for everyone. Derrick Bell wrestles with that problem in everything he writes. In *Faces at the Bottom of the Well,* he attributes this answer to Erin Edmonds, a former student:

> It is not a matter of choosing between the pragmatic recognition that racism is permanent no matter what we do, or an idealism based on the long-held dream of attaining a society free of racism. Rather, it is a question of both. Both the recognition of the futility of action—where action is more civil rights strategies destined to fail—and the unalterable conviction that something must be done, that action must be taken.

As Laura Banks, one of the women in the book, told me, "We have a long ways to go before we get home."

< Acknowledgments

I have many people to thank for their support and encouragement during this project and before. I especially want to acknowledge:

Abe Rochlin, my dad, who for his entire life has inspired three generations of relatives and friends by his honesty, integrity, and humor;

The people who allowed me to come into their lives with my tape recorder and personal questions. To a person, they shared important, hopeful, and sometimes painful memories with the optimistic wish that their life stories would encourage others to continue their education;

Sheila Slaughter, who provided constant encouragement and believed in my project while she demonstrated, by example, with John Taylor and Celestino Fernandez, the importance of maintaining the highest academic standards;

Gail Rochlin, my wife, who served as a guide, editor, and best friend, during the writing process;

Seth Rochlin, my son, who was my ultimate reality check;

Bruce Crowell, who has been part of my life as a mentor, friend and advisor for more than twenty-five years;

Martin Ahumada, a teacher and friend, who convinced me this project was possible;

Bob Tindall, whose message is that we are capable of greater accomplishments than we imagine;

Marge Anderson and Gerald McCoy, teachers who taught me the power and beauty of the written and spoken word;

Keith Kumm, a friend for a quarter of a century, and Dan Huff, my partner in writing, photography, and philosophy;

Fred and Harriet Rochlin, who have always inspired me by their curiosity about everything around them;

Karin Ranta, who transcribed nearly 2,000 pages of taped interviews;

Kent Rollins and the staff of the Arizona Alumni Association, who offered humor and perspective every step of the way.

race
& class
on campus

1 <

A Question of College

Fourth of July weekend, 1993. I was with Gail, my wife, at my twenty-fifth high school reunion at the Americana Hotel in Nogales, Arizona, a border town. Because of the peso's weakness and the economy in general, both the Americana and Nogales were struggling through hard times. But it was good to be home. It was good to see old friends and acquaintances for the first time in five, ten, and in some cases, twenty-five years.

We made the hour-long drive from Tucson and arrived early for the dinner-dance and reception. Annabelle Arias, Anna Sylvia Enciso, and Elizabeth de la Osa were at the check-in table, jotting down the names of returning members of the Nogales High School class of 1968. I got some hugs and kisses along with my name tag.

Seeing the three women sitting there, I began thinking about what their lives might have been like if they had moved away from Nogales, and about how things had changed, or hadn't changed, in twenty-five years. I thought about what these successful women might have accomplished if they'd gone to college.

I met Annabelle in first grade. She was a star even then, smart, involved, popular, and attractive. She did well on tests. Nogales is a small town, and we all knew who performed above or below grade level in various subjects. It must be tough for a kid to realize that some folks in Iowa don't think you measure up.[1] Annabelle didn't have that problem. She made the honor roll every six weeks and was a cheerleader.

A lot of the Mexican American girls got married out of high school and started having children. Annabelle's oldest was now twenty-two. Several of my classmates were grandparents. The guys often joined the Marines after graduation, and some went to Cochise Community College in nearby Douglas. The more ambitious attended Northern Arizona University or Arizona State University.

But the thought of an out-of-state college or university simply wasn't part of the equation in our world, and few of my Hispanic classmates even considered the University of Arizona. Even back then, I wondered why.

Annabelle, smart as she was, didn't go to college. Neither did Elizabeth or Anna Sylvia, another honor student in high school. But Armando Alfaro and Gilbert Gonzalez both went to the University of Arizona. Armando is a plastic surgeon in Tucson now. Gilbert eventually completed both a Ph.D. and a medical degree and is on the faculty at Harvard Medical School.

In the banquet room, a disc jockey played songs from the 1960s and *mariachi* music from the ages. Only in Nogales could Jimi Hendrix and the Rolling Stones mix perfectly with the brass and *guitarras* of a Mexican classic. This was the warmup act for the band that would crank up at about 8:30 p.m. You could talk until then.

A man and his wife approached Gail and me. He was tentative as he smiled and extended his hand in greeting. It wasn't one of these slap-on-the-back howdies. We weren't really friends in school, but we knew each other. I recognized his wife, too. He was quiet in school, not an athlete or one of the macho types I could've done without. He was thin in those days and hadn't gained an ounce since. His skin was a rich brown, his hair straight, black, parted on the left, and slick with Brylcream. His body was almost lost inside an over-sized pin-striped jacket. He looked like a forty-three-year-old teen-ager who'd borrowed his dad's clothes for a date.

"Hi, Jay. You probably don't remember me."

"Sure I do. How you been doing?"

"Great. You remember my wife then."

"Heck, yeah," I lied. "Long time. This is my wife, Gail."

Gail learned a long time ago that I am severely disabled when it comes to remembering names. She piped up. "I'm sorry, I didn't catch your names."

"I'm Richard Valenzuela. This is my wife, Connie."

Richard turned to me. "I hear you work at the university. Pretty good."

"I really like it there. It seems like I get to meet and talk to someone interesting nearly every day."

We chatted about jobs and children, mostly children. At my tenth reunion, Gail and I didn't have kids, and in this group that meant we didn't have a lot to talk about. By my twenty-fifth reunion we were the parents of a seven-year-old boy. Now we fit in. Now we could relate.

"Well, you know, our daughter that I mentioned . . ." Richard glanced at his shoes. I did, too. His had a perfect shine. Mine didn't.

"Yeah. You said she's going to be a senior."

"She's thinking about going to college. Maybe even the university."

"That's great. If there's anything I can do, let me know. I've gotten good at playing the bureaucracy up there."

"I wanted to ask you, do you think she can make it?"

"I don't know. What's she like? How's she doing in school?"

"She's kind of quiet, but she's strong." He smiled to himself and shook his head proudly. "She's a good girl. She works as a book-keeper over at Capin's Department Store after school and on Saturdays. She gets along there pretty well."

Richard had avoided answering my question. So I took a chance and pressed him. "So how does she do in her classes?"

"Oh, she's gotten a couple of Bs. She got a C once."

"And the rest were As?"

"Yes."

"Great. How about test scores? Has she taken the ACT or SAT?"

"She hasn't gotten her scores yet. They tell us she does well on those kinds of tests."

"Does she like school?"

"Yeah. She enjoys writing. She likes her math classes. She's good with numbers."

"Well, if she's thinking about college, why not encourage her to give it a try?"

Richard looked at Connie. It was obvious this was a conversation they'd had before.

"We agree with you," Richard said. "We've always made education important at home. But she's kind of anxious. And so are we, probably more than her. She's never really been away from home. She's not the kind of girl that, you know, automatically fits in. She can hold her own once she's comfortable and feels she has a place. We've heard that's not that easy at the U. And about money. We'd be able to help her a little, but we have two more coming up."

"She'll have to do her part for sure, but it's worth it."

"There's something else. I know this is a bad time to talk, but . . . "

Richard paused and looked at his shoes again. He wasn't sure about what he wanted to say, and he wasn't sure how I'd take it. Finally he looked up at me and began.

"It's just that, well, she's grown up around *mexicanos*.[2] Here in Nogales, just like me and Connie. Our people. We're comfortable here. We belong here. We speak Spanish when we want to. Our friends know automatically what our *¿cómo se dice?* expressions mean. We've never had to explain who we are. Except for her teachers, a few friends, and one or two people at the store, she's never really been around *americanos*. You know what I mean?"

"I think so."

"I hear that's a real different place, the university. We know she has what it takes up here in her head." Richard tapped his temple. "But how about the rest?"

I knew what he meant, and it made me think about Annabelle and Anna Sylvia. They also had what it took as far as brains. But they married just after high school and became homemakers in Nogales. Their husbands are both successful and earn good livings. Their children excel academically and in sports, and Annabelle's oldest daughter is active in student government. They've had good lives.

I also thought about Sylvia Alvarez, my girlfriend during my senior year. She did go on to college. I imagine her mom and dad graduated from high school, but I never knew for sure, and it didn't matter. Sylvia was quiet and didn't have a lot of buddies, just a fairly close circle of good friends. She wasn't a cheerleader, an athlete, or involved in organized high school activities. She had olive skin, dark eyes, and a smile that wouldn't quit. She was the youngest of three kids. I think her brother went off to the service. Her sister, the middle child, gave junior college a try, didn't finish, and if I recall correctly, went to secretarial school. At home, Sylvia's parents seemed more comfortable speaking Spanish, although when I was around they spoke English as a courtesy.

Commencement was held in the gym. We chose partners for the

procession. Sylvia and I marched together, along with 160 class-mates, to the music of "Pomp and Circumstance." Five hundred proud parents, grandparents, brothers, sisters, other relatives, teachers, and friends looked on. Teachers lined us up for the procession in order of our class rank. Sylvia was among the top five, so we went to the head of the line. If we'd been positioned by my ranking, we would have wound up somewhere in the mediocre middle. I remember thinking how distinguished and beautiful Sylvia looked with a blue National Honor Society sash draped over her white gown.

Back then, if you were a guy going into the service and had a girlfriend, you got married. It was almost a rule. If you were going to college, you broke up with your sweetheart, another rule. I think Sylvia and I broke up that night or a little later. It was time to start new lives. That summer, my friend Steve Smith and I gathered up our plastic hippie beads, hitchhiked to Haight-Ashbury in San Francisco, and began our post-high-school education by learning as much as we could about free love, LSD, Janis Joplin, and the Grateful Dead.

Sylvia entered the University of Arizona to get her English and Humanities requirements out of the way. She graduated with honors and went on to earn a master's degree in counseling. Her last name now is Hauser. She lives in New Jersey.

As I stood in the Americana Hotel that night, listening to one of those beautiful, wailing Mexican songs, I wondered why Sylvia went on to complete two college degrees, while so many of our friends stayed home? I wondered, but I didn't have an answer.

"I hear what you're saying, Richard. Tell you what. If your daughter is willing, I'd love to talk to her about the university. Here's my card. It's got my office and home numbers on it. Have her give me a call."

"Thanks. Her name is Gabriela."

2 <

The College Idea

I was in my office when the phone rang. The voice on the other end was soft and distant, a young woman's voice.

"Hello. Is this Mr. Rochlin?"

"Uh-huh. Who's this?"

"Gabriela Valenzuela."

I got a mental picture of Richard and the party at the Americana.

"My dad gave me your card. From the reunion last summer. He said it'd be okay to call."

I liked her right away. She was polite and serious. But she was nervous, too, and seemed to need time to get comfortable. That was fine with me. We chatted about Nogales. I made sure she was calling on my free 800 line.

"Anyway, Mr. Rochlin, I've been thinking a lot lately. About college."

"Your dad said you were interested."

"I always hoped I could go, but I don't know, I'm scared. I've been working part-time as a bookkeeper at Capin's Department Store. I'm sure they'd put me on full-time when I graduate high school. They like me over there."

She was clearly proud of what she did. It was in her voice. And she was a success at it. But she didn't call to talk about bookkeeping. I waited.

"I've been having these daydreams about college. As far back as I can remember. I keep trying to push it out of my mind because I just don't think it can happen."

"Why do you think that?"

"I don't know. It just seems so . . . far off."

I was thinking about some of my female classmates from Nogales, the smart ones who didn't go to college. And there was that question again—why? I thought about those who did, too, and what compelled them to take the leap.

"Gabriela, do you know how the idea of college got in your mind in the first place?"[1]

"Not really. Maybe from teachers and some of my friends who're going to college. I'm not sure. My parents, they always put my education on the top of the list of important things, but they only graduated high school. I don't think they expected me to keep going, except to take a few classes at Pima.[2] Until this summer, they wouldn't let me work because they were afraid it might hurt my grades. But last year I took some exam to tell whether I could make it. I did well."

"That doesn't surprise me." Already I could tell she was smart. She reminded me of Sylvia. But I knew the idea had to come from a specific place. I asked again. She thought for a long time.

"There's one thing I can think of. My great-grandfather used to tell stories about a niece of his. He was really proud of her. She became a lawyer and was always helping other people."

"Really?"

"Uh-huh. But my history is pretty iffy. Are you sure it's okay if we take this much time to talk?"

"Sure. Tell me about your great-grandfather."

"He came to Nogales with the 25th Infantry about 1918."

Her date was right on target. Camp Nogales was established in 1910. The name was changed to Camp Stephen D. Little in honor of a soldier who died in a border skirmish with Mexico in 1915. The U.S. Army moved the white soldiers out and replaced them with the all-black 25th in 1918. The black troopers were called Buffalo Soldiers. Camp Little remained segregated until it was shut down in 1931.[3]

I cut her off. I had to know. "Was your great-grandfather black?"

"Yeah, he was," she answered matter-of-factly. "He married a Mexican woman from Nogales, started a family. After the service, he found a job at a hardware store and spent the rest of his life here."

"He sounds like a special guy. You were lucky to know him."

"He was. He died just a couple of years ago. He was ninety-five, never went to college. I don't know if he graduated high school. But he read all the time. He was a serious amateur astronomer. He knew what was going on in the world, big time. We did a lot of stuff together. It's strange talking about him now. Last Sunday, for the first time since he died, I went to visit his grave. It was weird. I sort of spaced out staring at his headstone." A pause. "I wonder if he's why I decided to call you today?"

"Gabriela, do you have any spare time to read?"

"Ah, sure." She seemed a little confused by my abrupt change of topic. "I'm caught up on my work at school."

"Okay. Do you have something to write with?"

"Yes."

"Go to a library and get a book by Derrick Bell. It's called *And We Are Not Saved.* Just read the introduction and the prologue if that's all you have time for. We'll talk again soon. I want to hear what you think."

I didn't have to wait long. About a week later I had a voice-mail message:

"Mr. Rochlin, I wanted to get back to you this morning. Thanks for turning me on to that book. I read part of it and like it. But the reason I am calling, we're going shopping in Tucson on Saturday. Would you be willing to meet and talk about that book? And college? And . . . stuff. I hate talking on these machines. Anyway, ah, anytime's fine. We should get to Tucson about 9:30. If you call my dad at work and let him know, he'll get me to wherever you say. Thanks."

The timing of my first meeting with Gabriela Valenzuela couldn't have been better. Over the previous two years, I'd conducted interviews with nearly fifty Mexican American and African American graduates and "almost graduates" of the University of Arizona about making it through college as minorities.

Only recently did I begin to understand what they said. They weren't talking about advisors or theme dorms or class size. Their stories and experiences, covering eight decades, were about racism, money, and social class. Their stories were also about heroic parents who recognized that they and their children might indeed be victims of past and current racial and class discrimination. But they also embraced the notions of delayed gratification, hard work, individual sacrifice, and formal education as the way for their children to succeed in America.[4]

Most of my African American informants knew early in their lives that college would be part of their futures, no matter the cost.[5] Even though many of the older ones had been exposed to severe forms of racism, as had their parents, they didn't focus on it or think of themselves as victims. It was the future, not the past, that interested them.

In stark contrast to the Mexican Americans I interviewed, a significant number of the African Americans had at least one parent with some college education, if not a degree.[6] Still, those parents were generally underemployed. They knew the economic and personal toll the pursuit of an education would entail, but they possessed an almost religious faith that college offered the only path to a secure and prosperous future.

Many of my Mexican American informants also knew early that college would be part of their plans. But the message wasn't as clear.[7] While highly valuing education, their parents had no experience with formal educational institutions and virtually none with colleges and universities.[8]

At the same time that I was conducting these interviews, I was reading authors who were part of a new movement called critical race theory. Among them were Derrick Bell,[9] Richard Delgado,[10] Kimberly Crenshaw,[11] and Patricia Williams.[12] For the first time since I began my exploration of "the literature," hoping to find at least a framework for understanding the minority experience in higher education, I heard voices that rang true. I was captivated by Derrick Bell and his fictional colleague, friend, and alter ego, Geneva Crenshaw.

These writers have created a new scholarship built on the need to examine issues such as race, class, and gender in ways academics haven't tried before. They argue that stories, parables, chronicles, and music, as well as the actual voices of the minority individuals being studied, offer valuable insights that formal scholarship misses.

It was exciting for me to discover the critical race theorists. I felt they might help America step in a new direction on this divisive matter. I wanted Gabriela to be in on it, or at least aware of their ideas.

Saturday morning. I got to my office early, planning to knock off a few hours of work at the computer. It didn't happen. I managed to pass the time just fine, but my fingers barely touched the keyboard.

The rapping at the window startled me. It was Richard and Gabriela, with their faces pressed against the glass. They were laughing and trying not to be too obvious about it. They must've knocked on the window several times before I noticed. What is it they say about first impressions?

I knew I'd been caught, smiled back at them, and motioned toward the door. As soon as my feet hit the floor I had a sinking feeling in my gut about what I was doing. First, in my study, I was attempting to apply nontraditional qualitative analysis to the poignant life experiences of fifty people who knew a lot more about being black or Mexican American at the university than I did. As if that wasn't presumptuous enough, now I had to figure out what on earth I would say to encourage Gabriela to give college a try.

I took some wisdom from the folks I'd interviewed and decided that whether she knew it or not, Gabriela's decision to go to college had been made a long time ago. It was just a matter of helping her see that.

I opened the door and introduced myself. We spoke for a moment: it was awkward, as most first meetings are. We decided that Richard would head off to the hardware store, while Gabriela and I walked to a nearby coffee house to talk. We agreed to meet Richard back at my office at noon. I got a real sense of how important this meeting was to Richard by the handshake he gave as he left. It was his second of the day, and it made me wonder if I'd ever see my fingers again. I think he was telling me, in the only way he knew how, that he was trusting me with his daughter's future. But more than that he wanted me to understand his frustration at being unable to provide the advice and counsel Gabriela needed himself.

It was up to me, he was saying. I wanted to tell him, "It's okay, Richard. Gabriela's going to make it. You and your wife have already done your parts well."

Gabriela was tall, like her dad, and she moved well for a teenager. She wasn't awkward. She had a grace about her, an athleticism. Her face was bright and hopeful, especially her brown eyes. She had black hair that hung to her shoulders, and she kept tugging at the ends of it. Nerves. She had a certain manner, an eagerness that came from more than being seventeen. I could sense her desire to talk, and on the way to the Student Union coffee bar, we did.

She had a good grasp of Derrick Bell's ideas. She understood his analysis of the intractability of the problem of race in America. But she didn't buy what she described as his sense of hopelessness, his belief that racism was permanent. We gave our orders. The talk got serious when our coffee came. Gabriela sipped a cup of French roast as she spoke.

"I've seen it happen plenty of times," she said. "If you have a goal, focus, and work twice as hard as the next person, you're going to make it.[13] You just need to know what you want to do."

Listening to her, I wondered if there was a Spanish equivalent for Pollyanna. But I held my tongue.

"Bell would wonder why, if you're right, so many whites seem to make it, while so few blacks or Hispanics do? If I read him right, he's saying that millions of blacks and Hispanics do focus, do have goals, work hard, and still don't have as much of a chance of achieving what they might have if they'd been born white."

Gabriela stared at me. I had a sip of my Kona and waited, expecting her to respond. When she didn't, I pushed the point.

"Gabriela, come on, Bell is an optimist compared to some of the others. If you want to read a really depressing book about racial problems, try Andrew Hacker's *Two Nations: Black and White, Separate, Hostile, Unequal.*"[14]

At that her shoulders sank. She studied the inside of her coffee cup. Good job, Rochlin, I thought to myself. This is a seventeen-year-old you're talking to, not a seminar-hardened graduate assistant. Don't come on so strong.

I knew she had a good point. The people I spoke with confirmed many of the general themes of critical race theory, but they also supported the tenets of minority conservatives such as Shelby Steele, Stephen Carter, Thomas Sowell, and Richard Rodriguez.[15]

Their insights were startlingly simple and extremely complex at the same time. Most, including for the moment my new friend, Gabriela, agreed with Stephen Carter: "The only change for which we can reasonably hope will come about because we commit ourselves to battle for excellence, to show ourselves able to meet any standard, to pass any test that looms before us, in short, to form ourselves into a vanguard of black professionals who are simply too good to ignore."[16]

Shelby Steele put it this way: "There will be no end to despair and no lasting solution to any of our problems until we rely on individual effort within the American mainstream—rather than collective action against the mainstream—as our means of advancement."[17]

I'd decided something about Gabriela. She had a lively mind and wanted badly to be taken seriously as she tried out some new ideas. But few things are as fragile as the confidence of a seventeen-year-old. I don't think she expected to hear a dissenting opinion, at least not so soon. We had to get more comfortable with each other first. I needed to listen. She needed to talk. The tough stuff, the parts where the world doesn't quite add up, could come later.

"You know, Gabriela, a whole lot of very smart folks agree with you."

She pulled her nose out of her coffee mug. I had her attention again.

"Let me buy you another cup." I waved the waiter over and ordered. "Let's talk about you and college."

"College," she said with a sigh, and was back pulling at her hair. "I really want to go. I do. But I don't know what it's going to be like. My parents really can't afford to support me, and I don't know if I'll be able to work and make the grades I need to stay in school. At the same time, I know I need to do it . . ."

"Whoa!" I interrupted. "Let me tell you, lots of people before you have had those exact thoughts and still made it through college."

"But how?"

"Lots of ways. Listen, I've been working on a project. What do you say we go back to my office?"

"What about the coffee?"

"We'll get it to go. I want you to meet some folks. Well, sort of meet them."

She shrugged and gave me a look, like maybe I should try the decaf next time. I paid the check. On the way out we walked through an open-air patio lined with newspapers, many of them free. They covered every special interest, outdoor activity, and political and social cause imaginable. Gabriela scooped up as many as she could carry.

"I can read these on the ride home," she said.

We sat at the meeting table in my office. I told her about my study and how most of the people I interviewed knew early in life they'd be going to college, even though they generally came from poor families. And I explained how other factors, such as exposure to coaches and military service, influenced them, too. I fiddled with my tape recorder as I spoke.

"Some of these people sound a lot like you. Want to hear some of them?"

She was peeling the lid from her cup. Steam billowed out. "Sure."

I started her out with Laura Nobles Banks. She was as eloquent as anybody I met, an energetic and strong black woman who, over the course of three decades, was one of Tucson's strongest voices for racial equality, especially in the schools. I pressed the play button.

Laura Banks, 1943

> College had always been in my mind. It had not been an option. It was a mandate for us as far back as I can remember. My older brother went to college. He started here at the university, James Nobles, Jr.,[18] and went to Wiley College in Marshall, Texas. That's where he graduated.

Education was something that our family held in high esteem. The kids were going to get a college education. It was a mandate.

I had one brother that went to Tuskegee to learn how to be a tailor and he had his own shop in Los Angeles. Jimmy went and graduated. Pearl went but never graduated. I went and Rosalee didn't. Almost all my cousins at least started.

I can't say the university was a motivating factor for me to go on. It was other influences. The university itself definitely was not. But that was the means to which I could get what I needed to get. That was to become an educated person.

I pushed the stop button. We sipped our coffees for a moment, thinking over what Laura Banks had said. Every time I listened to the tapes, I was struck again at the consistency of experience—nearly everyone knew that college would be part of their lives from an early age.[19]

We still had a while before Richard arrived. I suggested taking Gabriela on a trip from the 1930s to the 1990s to show how the words and ideas kept repeating themselves regardless of the decade. The first group consisted exclusively of African Americans.

Elgie Mike Batteau, 1935

The idea of college was always part of my life.[20] I always wanted to go. That was my idea to go to college, to finish college. My mother pressed that because she didn't have a chance to even go through public school.

Mildred Hudson McKee, 1940

Education was so important that I didn't think life could start until I went to college. I was so brainwashed. The idea that I would go to college was always a part of my growing up.[21]

Anna Jolivet, 1950, 1965, 1972

College was always a part of my plans. Always. Not a question of "Will I?," it was just a matter of my making that a part of my plans. After my sophomore year I signed up for additional science and math classes. My counselor called me in after school started and said, "I don't understand why you are taking these courses."

I asked, "Is that a problem?"

She said, "Well, you got chemistry and physics. You don't need all of those programs, those classes."

I replied, "Well, if I go to the university, I have to have them."

She said, "You're wasting your time. You should be taking home-making, some sewing and cooking, learning how to take care of a home because that is the kind of work that you are going to be able to get. You're not going to be able to go to the university."

I said, "I have no interest in the cooking or sewing classes and it is my intention to take the courses that I have outlined. And I do plan to go to the university."

She spent a bit of time talking to me about why I was wasting my time and should not be pursuing such interests.

Finally when she realized that I was not about to change my mind, and I knew that my mother would not tell me to make a change, she said, "Well, you're making a mistake. But you go ahead, you're just making a mistake. You're not going to be able to get anything to do when you finish school."[22]

That was the counselor, and the same counselor did the same thing in counseling my younger brother when he came along.

Olden Lee, 1968

My parents pushed the idea of college. From grade school. My great-aunt was a schoolteacher. She was very close to the family and pretty much said, you all ought to go to college and let me tell you why and on and on.

Lisa Watson, 1983

The idea of college was always there because my sisters and brothers were in college. I always looked up to them. I started hanging out with higher achievers.[23]

I started taking college prep courses at Catalina High. I knew that is what I wanted to do: I wanted to go to college.

Robin Lemon, 1983

It was assumed for all of us that we would go to college. We realized that even though you may have other talents, you needed a college education to get anywhere.

As soon as I pressed the stop button, Gabriela asked a question. "How come you only let me listen to black people?"

A good observation. She didn't miss much.

"I guess because their responses to that part of the interview were so consistent. Education was highly valued in their families, their parents wanted them to go to college, they expected to go, and in spite of some difficult obstacles, they did and succeeded."

"Are you saying that Mexican American parents don't value college as much as African American parents?"[24]

"Of course not. But at least among the people I spoke to, the idea of college wasn't as crystal clear."

I wanted to keep going, but Richard arrived. I greeted him at the door and ushered him into my office. I explained what we were doing and invited him to take part in the discussion. Looking back, I guess it was a gamble. For one thing, Gabriela might have felt inhibited, talking in front of her dad. I didn't know how Richard would take it either. It wasn't like we were close friends, and the issues and experiences we were kicking around got pretty personal.

I knew the gamble worked when I asked Richard if he'd ever considered college. He couldn't wait to get himself into a chair and start talking. Gabriela's eyes widened a bit. She was surprised at her dad's willingness to open up. She wanted to listen.

"Of course, yes, I thought about it," Richard said. "But I never thought it was possible. I wish I'd at least given it a try. Now I do."

"Did it come up in your family at all?"

"My parents cared about education, but couldn't really guide me. My mom and dad never finished high school. For them, my earning a high school diploma was a major thing.[25] They cried at my graduation, I remember that like yesterday. For most of the people watching, I was just one more brown face in the second half of the line, but for my mom and dad, boy, I was accomplishing the American dream."

Gabriela beamed at her father's recollections. It occurred to me that she'd probably never heard them before. She smiled into her coffee.

"But high school was it," Richard said. "I don't know why, exactly. I guess it was as far as my parents could see. Come to think of it, I don't remember my counselor or any teacher ever talking to me about it either."

I asked Richard about Gabriela and college. Richard fixed his eyes on his daughter, then looked away. He folded his hands on the table and sighed.

"I'm not so sure," he began. "It's not easy to say these things. The schooling, the opportunity, it would be wonderful. But I'm afraid for her. I've heard stories. It's not so good for a Mexican girl. She would be hurt if it didn't work out. But, yes, we want it for her, Gabi's mother and I. Very, very badly."

Richard looked at Gabriela again. He was grinding his hands together so tightly his skin was turning pale.

"I think we want it so badly because we didn't have it. Do you see?"

Gabriela's eyes filled with tears. She was looking at her father. He turned to her and their stares locked. Then he coughed into his hand and looked at me. I think he wanted me to rescue him, to get onto something lighter. But I was caught up in the moment, too. It occurred to me that the payoff from a long research project isn't transcribing tapes or the drudgery of writing a long report that will eventually take up space on a library shelf. It's times like this.

Gabriela spoke first. "How about letting my dad hear some of your tapes? You said you also interviewed some Mexican Americans."

"Heck, yeah." I was delighted to switch the focus to the tape recorder. "But it's noon. Sure you don't want lunch first?"

"If you guys can hold out, so can I," said Richard. "I've always wondered why some *mexicanos* go to college and get the good jobs and others don't. Maybe I'll learn something. No?"

"If you figure out the answer to that let me know and quickly," I said.

Carlos Vélez-Ibáñez, 1961, 1968

I had the idea of college in my mind when I was five years old. We used to take Sunday drives around Tucson. One day, when I was five we were coming around the university area. It was dusk. I still remember. It's like a picture. They had much brighter lights then. The university really lit up. Most of the buildings here, the library, the museum was built in front. Douglass, Old Main.

I asked my dad, "¿Qué es eso?" You know, look at all these buildings. What are they?

He said, "Bueno, ahí está todo la sabiduría del mundo." Well, there exists all the knowledge in the world.

And I said, "Bueno, voy a trabajar ahí." I want to work there.

I knew when I was five that I was going to do something other than digging a ditch. The notion of university was born very early on because my dad put it in such a way that he created a template in my brain. I'm sure.

When he said to me, "Bueno, ahí está todo al sabiduría del mundo," it stimulated me to think that I could have access to it. That was the template. That was his contribution.

I had no idea about what it meant. He laid a mythic template down. It was a drive from my house. It was not on the other side of the moon. It wasn't anything unrecognizable. What was different was the physical surroundings. It wasn't something so strange that I couldn't have a relationship to it. All my dad had to do was drive there. All I had to do is put the car in gear, and I am here.

I had no idea when I came here as a seventeen-year-old kid, of how this worked, why it worked, when it worked, what it meant. None of that. I didn't even know what a unit meant.

This is 1956. I came here and I took nineteen semester units. Everything from chemistry through accounting, you name it. First semester freshman year with pimples on my face and a crew cut. One of fifty Mexicans on this entire campus. There were probably 6,000 students then.

That was when you were still called "boy" by seniors. I remember they even had us wear a beanie, which I refused to wear. I even painted the A.[26]

Mary Ott, 1935

I remember every night we sat around the dining room table and we did our homework until it was done. Both parents were absolutely sure that was the only way we would get anywhere, since we had no background. My mother's side of the family was newcomers to the area. I was absolutely going to go to college. I was Mexican only part of the time, and I had one or two Mexican friends who also went to college. It was Mary Ott who was going to go. Certainly my father was part of it. He was a very well-read man. And my mother had gone to a private girls' school with all the nuns and that sort of thing. I don't remember ever thinking I was not going to college.

Robert Figueroa, 1948

I used to hear about friends who were automatically going to the university. It was their lifestyle to think about the U of A. When I heard of this, I also wanted to go to college, but I didn't know how I was going to do it.

I carried the *Tucson Citizen*.[27] I was a paper boy for two years. Then I carried the *Star*[28] for another two years.

I used to deliver papers to O'Rielly Motors on Sixth Avenue. One day, I walked in there to deliver a paper to Mr. Stewart. I don't remember his first name. He said, "Bob, you're getting on in age. Are you going to go to college?"

I said, "Oh no, I don't have the money to go."

"You didn't answer my question. Would you like to go to the university?"

"Of course I would. Who wouldn't?"

"Well," he said. "Here's how you can go to the university. Go to the registrar's office and talk to a lady by the name of Stewart who happens to be my wife."

He informed me that I could get a loan to pay for my tuition for the semester on the condition that I paid it back before the semester was over. While Mrs. Stewart was going through my school records, she discovered that I had not taken the required college entrance courses. It was then necessary for me to go back and take geometry and algebra. I was already a junior or senior in high school. I went back to get those two classes. I had to stay over by half a year because I was working all the time.

Finally, I got to the university, and by that time, my brothers had gotten married. I had one sister and an aunt, whom I helped support.

Something else happened. While I was stationed at Camp Crowder, Missouri, one Sunday morning a car stopped in front of the chapel and an elderly lady, about sixty-three or so (I'm ten years older than that now!) got out. She was trying to get some books from the trunk of her car into the chapel but was having difficulty lifting them. I volunteered to help her. She invited me to her home in Joplin, and both she and her husband were very kind to me. I told them that when the war was over I was going to come back just to say hello.

Well, when I got home I had a letter from her saying, "Robert, where do you want to go to school?"

I said, "What are you talking about?"

She said, "I want to send you through whatever school you want to attend."

I said, "I'd like to go to the U of A."

Would you believe she sent me $3,000? That was a lot of money in 1946. I tried to repay the loan, but she wouldn't take any money from me. Believe me, that helped tremendously. I was still working, but that helped a lot. That's what enticed me to get married.

I got married to Hortense Preciado, a girl from Yuma, during my senior year at the university. She promised me faithfully that she was going to work to help me finish. We were married thirty-three years before she passed away.

Marty Cortez, 1958

My dad was a very quiet man, few words but really strong in his beliefs. We never doubted that we would continue our schooling. He would always say, "Well, when you go to school and pursue a career," or "when you go to the university."

He was very liberal in the sense that he always said that regardless of what you think your life is going to be like as you get older, you need your education because that is the one thing you will never lose.

I started thinking about college pretty much when I entered high school, because he said to be sure that I did whatever I needed to do in order to prepare myself to go on to college or university.

I was the first kid in the family to go to college,[29] so there wasn't anybody else within the family to talk about what is it like or what to do. I just knew I was going to college and I needed to figure out how to do that.

Richard Gonzales, 1972, 1975

College was integral to the messages our parents were giving us. They kept drilling from day one that we would go to college. They saw their mission as getting us to the college doors for that first year. The commitment we gave our parents was that we would go to college that first year. If we chose to drop out, then that was our choice. But we were not going to fail to attend college and then have as an excuse that we were never given the opportunity.

At Sunnyside High[30] in 1968, my peer group was not considered likely to succeed. By that time, I was thinking about what I wanted to major in in college. I thought I would go to my counselor about it. When I went to see him, I got an aptitude form that tried to figure out where your strengths lay. It asked you questions, and you answered them by punching a hole and when you folded the thing up, by reading the pin marks, you figured out the aptitudes you had.[31]

All you had to know was how to read the English language to be able to read the form. It scored me high in sciences and social studies and math, history and things of that nature. So I was sitting there with Mr. Patton. I began the conversation with I didn't know what I wanted to do on down the road. I didn't tell him that I took the test in order to figure out what I was going to major in.

So he looks and nods his head and seems to be reading it and asks me if I had ever considered carpentry, that I really wasn't college material and that college really wasn't for me, that I really should get into something like a vocational course and work with my hands.

I told him I considered carpentry. He asked me if I had been in wood shop. I told him, yes, I had been in wood shop my freshman year and that if he looked at my record, he would see a notation from Mr. Wismer that he never wanted me to be in his wood shop class ever again. At that point I figured what the hell, it just was not worth it here. I politely excused myself and left and that was it.

Now in retrospect, I don't think Patton was doing it because he was a racist. I just think he didn't know any better. They felt in their own way that they were doing the right thing for us. I can tell you that this counselor did have a good heart. He just didn't know any better. He probably thought he was saving me from something. As with all of these other kids.

Tom Amparano, 1973, 1981

I started thinking about college when I was in elementary school. I remember the basketball coach. Dickie Martinez is now the principal of Menlo Park Elementary. He was the first Hispanic I knew that had even gone or even told me what the University of Arizona was.

I couldn't even pronounce it. It was OO-AY or something like that when I first heard about it. Finally I got that it was U of A. That was when I first started thinking about the university. In elementary school.

College was beyond my parents' world.[32] They just wanted us to do good and graduate from Tucson High and get a decent job. Stay out of trouble, be good citizens. That was their ambition. The lucky thing, I had the GI Bill. Plus, I had the incentive of a wife and kid I had to take care of. The motivators were there.

Julieta Gonzalez, 1973

My parents were both involved in the PTA. They never missed a parent teacher conference even though my dad would work a lot of overtime and odd hours. Education was the single most important goal. Education was my goal in life. My dad started a savings account for my college education the day I was born. College was just an extension of another step in your education.

Evelia Martínez, 1975

The idea of college. I remember even in the sixth grade, there was a half a dozen kids that were the top students, and we would talk about what we wanted to be when we grew up. I wanted to be a teacher because I had some teacher that was a strong influence in my life. To me, that was the idea of a good job.

My mother valued education. For her, if she could give us the best education possible, then she would have done her job as a parent.

I had a variety of counselors, and at that point the counselors were saying to me, "Well, you're Mexican. Even if you graduate from high school, what you need to know is how to cook and how to sew because you're going to just go home and be pregnant and have kids."[33]

I had a freshman counselor who told me that, a man. "You're Mexican. You're not going to go to college. You know, what you need to learn is how to cook and sew."

I refused to take the schedule home for my mother to sign. I said, "I'm not taking this home. I need to take college prep courses." Back in junior high I knew I wanted to go to college.

I think back and ask what made me do it? It was because there was no other choice for me. I knew that I was going to have to get a good education so I could get a good job so that I could support my mother or support myself. It was always that kind of an issue.

Mike Duran, 1983, 1986

I think my parents aspired that I go to college. But I think, like a lot of parents today, they don't understand the process.[34]

The idea of college didn't really enter my mind until high school. Until I saw that Salpointe[35] was a definite feeder into the University of Arizona and other colleges. But it really wasn't until then that I recognized what college was all about, the importance of it.

I have to say that I think the philosophy at Salpointe was to move kids into college. I wouldn't really say that I was tracked, but I do recall the one or two times I visited with my counselor. It was she who said, "Well, gee, you are a Mexican American. Don't you want to be a carpenter, a cement finisher, a bricklayer, roofer?"

I looked at her and said, "Why? Those jobs are hard. You work outdoors. Why would I want to do that? I want to go to college and use my head."

"Oh, no, no. College isn't for you. You don't have the grades. You don't have the test scores."

I didn't know what she meant. I didn't understand what she was saying to me at the time. That actually happened to me at Salpointe. And it happened to others. Other Mexican American children that I knew.

I still have the little bench I made in wood shop. It's not a work of art. That was 1972 and 1973 when I was a senior in high school. I just looked at her and laughed and said, "You don't know what you're talking about," and we ended the conversation. I never spoke to her again.

I stopped the tape. It was well past 1:30 p.m. I was about to suggest lunch again, figuring everyone was famished. But Gabriela was fascinated by what she'd heard and wanted to talk about it.

"It really is discouraging," she said, "listening to what they went through. Hearing the actual voices, it makes it so real. Like they're here with us. But it's inspiring, too, the way they succeeded."

"It sure is."

"I see what you mean, the idea of college being different for the Mexican Americans. I guess if you don't have parents who're always on you about education, you might as well forget it. That's kind of scary."

I smiled. "It's easy to think that. But I found plenty of people who got into college a lot of different ways."

"Like how?"

"Coaches, sports scholarships, the GI Bill. There were guys, they went into the Marines and met someone who got them thinking they could go to college, and that was enough. A lot of times it's little things. Some folks got into college and got good educations because they could hit a baseball or run faster than anybody else."

"I knew a couple of track guys from Nogales," Richard said. "One of them went to Arizona State. Free."

"If you could run fast, that could've been you, Richard."

"Hey, I was a speedster. But only after I got my first car. A GTO, 1969. I rebuilt that car from hubcap to roof."

"Big engine, I bet," I said.

"Oh, serious power. Man, what a great ride." He gave Gabriela a stern look. "But you're always going to drive safe, right Gabi?" He looked back at me. "She just got her license."

Gabriela rolled her eyes. "I'll drive just the way you did, Dad."

Richard made a face and pressed his hands to his chest. "*Mi corazón.*"

We got a good laugh out of that. I readied the tapes. "Well, if you want to hear more . . . "

They did.

Richard Salvatierra, 1943, 1967

The idea of college wasn't necessarily a thought in my early life. The psychology with most Hispanic families was that you would go through high school and that would probably be enough.[36] Also there wasn't quite the same appreciation for higher education, perhaps because it wasn't quite as critical as it is in today's world.

Partly, my entree into college was my interest in sports, especially baseball. I was offered a baseball scholarship to come to the university. I accepted it.

Beginning to think about college had to do with the relationship I had with my mother, who was a very gentle, very understanding person. She seemed to always want to help her kids do whatever they wanted to do. I guess I was the first one to come along to even begin thinking in terms of wanting to go to college. I suppose it wasn't just a matter of sports.

Hadie Redd, 1955

I was recruited by Dr. Hazel Daniels. He's now passed away. He was a black doctor in Phoenix. He was very much interested in me attending the University of Arizona because he came to the university and played football here years before I did. He encouraged me to attend. Not only was it an excellent school academically but a good school sportswise.

College was on my mind. This was a part of the orientation received from my high school coach. He encouraged us all to prepare ourselves to go to college. He was more than a coach. He was an advisor to us. He tried to encourage all of us to go to college. I had many offers. To go to Cal. I must have had ten or fifteen letters. My mother has them some place. I could have gone back east. But I wanted to stay near my folks and attend school here in Arizona. I made that decision.

I knew it wasn't going to be easy, with the way things were, discrimination and all. But as a young eighteen- to nineteen-year-old, you can't see as much in depth as you can as an adult. You concentrate on your studies as much as you can and try to give your best on the floor or on the baseball field. I made the best decision in coming to the University of Arizona.

Malachi Andrews, 1955

I was the first person in my neighborhood that I knew of that went to college and graduated. No one ever told me to go to college.

At that time in the black community, if your mother was struggling and your dad died and there was eight kids, the atmosphere was, "Okay, your mother struggled all these years to help you in high school and you graduated. Now you owe your mother. You owe your mother to go out and get a job to help your mother with the younger ones." I was older and I was a boy.

College wasn't in my mind. I guess I'd heard about it, but I do not remember ever wanting to or ever talking about going to college until after I had graduated high school. I was good with my hands. The day of graduation, everybody would say, "Where you going?"

All of a sudden, Eugene was going to Los Angeles City College. He was going to be on the gymnastics team. Marcus was going over here to college. Everybody. The gymnastics athletes had got their grades, and they were all college prep. I was around them, but I didn't have the background, the counseling that they had. Gymnastics was an elite sport. So you had people pushing them to go to college.

We had a great track team. They were going to college. Everybody was going to college. And I didn't see no reason—I was just as smart as them in my mind. I had gotten As in art and won an art contest. I was the best artist in school. I was a member of the student council. I was the head cheerleader. I said, "Wait a minute." So I just went over to Los Angeles City College and got a catalogue. Just on my own.

I never got counseled to go to college. I wasn't college prep. I was in all the wood shops. I took wood shop 1, 2, 3. I was assistant teacher in high school. The teacher would just say, "Go ask Malachi." Metal shop I was good in. I got As in metal shop. I got As in drafting. And then when I did go to junior college, this lady says, "Why are you here?"

I says, "'Cause I wanna learn. I wanna go to college and get a degree. I guess that's what you're supposed to do?"

She said, "Yeah, but you work so good with your hands. You scored the highest in the whole school. You should be a carpenter. You could make a lotta money. You should go to trade school."

My first problem with a white person was that woman who told me to be a carpenter. I never went to another counselor.

I was at home one day, and the telephone rang, and Mom says this man wants to come over and talk to me. Somebody from Arizona, and he says he's in a college.

There was a knock at the door. Carl Cooper, who was the track coach at Arizona, came in with a briefcase and folder and he said, "Do you know why I'm here?"

"No."

He says, "I'm the track coach at the University of Arizona. I've been in L.A. recruiting, and I'd like to talk to you about the University of Arizona."

And I says, "Oh?" And I was caught by surprise.

He sat down on the couch and he opened his folder and he showed me pictures of the Old Main and a few things. You didn't have much around here then in 1953.

He said, "I want to bring you in. We are trying to get a track program going. We want to raise our level of participation in track and field to be competitive, and we're looking for a long jumper."

He says, "Here's all the papers. We'll help you fill it out. We can do it now." I filled it all out right there. I didn't care. I was going to school to graduate. I didn't care what school I went to.

Arnold Elias, 1959

When I was in high school, I remember being called in by my counselor. I was never a great student. But my counselor called me in and said that we had to map out your junior or senior year. She said, "What is it you want to do?"

And I said, "Well, I want to go to college." That is what my dad said and there was never any question about that. And if I came home and said that I had enrolled in something else, he would bring me back and say, "What's going on here?"

There was no question that this lady wanted me to be an auto mechanic or a cement finisher because the practicability of my going to the university and being successful, in her opinion, probably didn't exist.[37]

She tried very hard for me not to get involved in the college prep curriculum. "Why don't you take the course in auto mechanics or wood shop?"

I said, "No, no. I got to take these courses because that's what it takes to get you to college."

She did a whole lot of things to try to dissuade me. She finally agreed, well okay. It was done very reluctantly. I don't think she ever said, "You can't do that."

Now it kind of pisses me off. But on the other hand, she didn't know any better. There was a system.

Going to the university was still in my mind. A pro baseball career also occurred to me. In my senior year, when I graduated from high school, my dad encouraged me to go to a tryout camp. I hadn't been recruited by anyone, by any college. I was going to be a walk-on at the university. So he encouraged me to go to a tryout camp for the Cleveland Indians, and I did, and I got an offer to play ball.[38]

I was a minor and couldn't sign a contract, so I came home one day with this piece of paper. God, they were going to pay me to play ball.

When we sat down to talk, my dad asked me, "Where do they want you to go?" I said, "Well, I can't stay here. I have to go to Florida." And he said to me, "Well, they're going to pay $180 a month to play ball, and you're going to be gone, and you're not going to school. I don't think you better go, and I don't think you better sign, and I can't sign for you. You stay here and go to school."

I was just absolutely devastated. I had been on the field with people whose names you don't even remember, Gordon and Boudreau, who were the kingpins for the Cleveland Indians, and Luke Easter, guys I had been out there practicing with and then my dad said, "No, I don't think you better go."

I think that just knocked the stuffing out of me because I did enroll at the university, and I didn't do very well.

The only reason I went initially was because my dad said I had to go. But later on, when I made up my own mind, it coincided with those values that he had already set in my own mind. It was time to fish or cut bait.

Jim Garcia, 1975

I think my parents were really trying to push their work ethic. I think basically they felt it was important to do school. I don't think, at the time, you know like today, you and I might instill in our kids that, "Hey college is the next level, you don't stop at high school." I don't think my parents were pushing the college issue. I don't recall any of that happening, but I do recall that they said, "Hey, you know, school's very important. You will finish school, and you'll get that done."

The idea of college came to me by somebody who did hit me up one side of the head.[39] It was my tennis coach, Ed Nuñez, who is now the assistant principal at Pueblo. He basically said, "Look, guy, you've been seeing this girl for like four years now, and you're talking about marriage when you guys finish high school, and you're talking about this vocational program, and look at your status. You're taking all the right courses. You're already at college level math that you're registered in. You've taken all the entry-level courses to college."

I just didn't think college was in the cards. It wasn't going to happen. I just said no college, and then when he pursued it and banged on me some more, I said, "You know my parents can't afford it. It's not going to be an option and I'm going to do this vocational school for a year or two at $2,500 and I'm through with it." That's how much I knew about it at the time.

The university didn't cost anywhere near $2,500. It was $200 a semester. It was actually cheaper to come to the university for four years living at home than to spend $2,500 in this damn training school. And I was really hot on electronics. I really liked it. I had a great time with it. I got straight As and I was just having a good time.

So he says, "Well, you can be an engineer."

"Maybe so." That was the turning point right there.

Alfredo Márquez, 1948, 1951

My parents always emphasized education. They didn't want me to quit school. Unfortunately, at that time, most of the Mexican kids quit high school to go to work in the mill.[40] They had no plans to go to college. The family probably didn't encourage them. In my family, my cousins, we all finished high school and, basically, everyone went on with their education.

I had wanted to go to college. I always liked math and I always liked to fly. I had hoped to become an aeronautical engineer. I liked flying. I used to build a lot of model airplanes when I was a kid.

When I was in the service I began thinking of being an attorney. I had a friend of mine who was a Marine pilot. He and I were instructors together. Tommy Walsh was his name. He had gone to Loyola University in Chicago. He was going to be a priest. He was very well educated, which also gave me a great desire to further my education. He was bright. He was talking about going back. He had decided that he wasn't going to be a priest. He wasn't cut out for it. He and I talked a lot about what we were going to do afterwards. That's probably where I got the idea about going to law school.

Cressworth Lander, 1950

The idea of going to college was almost like something far off. The University of Arizona, although it is a state school, was almost viewed as a school for little rich kids from the east. I mean, people were not really recruited. People were not sought to go to the university in the 1930s and early 1940s.

I guess the big turnaround, as it relates to education and as it relates to the university and a number of other schools, was World War II and the GI bill. I think that the GI bill is probably the greatest single social service program or education program that was ever passed. It raised the standard of living of the entire nation in fifteen or twenty years. It certainly did a great service for blacks.

I probably would not have gone to college. I didn't say that I didn't think about college. I certainly didn't think that I would be able to go to the University of Arizona. The military made that possible. The Marine Corps. The U.S. Marine Corps.

John Huerta, 1955

College was not something I had given much thought to. Without a history of higher education in our background, it was difficult to understand the importance of higher education.[41] Expectations really never went beyond the high school level.

The Korean conflict broke out, and Uncle Sam began to mobilize. In August of 1950, we all went to the train station to see our classmates off to war. Within weeks, the Tucson detachment was part of an amphibious landing at Inchon, Korea, the biggest campaign of the war. The casualties were heavy, and they included four of my close friends from Barrio Hollywood.[42] It was a sad time for us in the neighborhood.

Within weeks, I was called in for a physical and quickly classified as a 1-A, meaning I was ready for the draft. Immediately, I started looking for alternatives. We found out that students enrolled in the Reserve Officer Training Corps, ROTC, program at the University would be classified as 3-A, service after graduation. More importantly, married students would be classified a 3-D, deferred. All of a sudden, the University of Arizona started to look better and better.

So many voices. We needed a breather. Gabriela suggested candy bars and sodas, and that sounded good. After a few minutes we were back at it, talking about college and listening to the tapes.

G. A. Larriva, 1929

> The idea of college. I didn't think I was going to make it. I was trying to figure how I was going to make it. One of my older sisters had gone to college. My father put her through. She went to UCLA. After that, we all wanted to go to college. We figured if we got a better education, we'd make more money. I got the scholarship and my father sent my brother with me.

Nazario Gonzales, 1935

> At the time, *mexicanos* went to college less often than other groups. That's tragic. We should have had somebody promoting it.
>
> The idea of college didn't occur to me until after I graduated from high school. I took a commercial course in high school. It seemed that was all you needed. I graduated from high school in 1932. I went out and worked for my father, and in 1934, I entered the university. Spent two years and started the third and had to quit. I went in and I wanted to take everything that was in that catalog, but I couldn't make it financially.

Frank Felix, 1971

> My parents never assumed I'd go to college. No, no. Never. They were happy that I graduated high school. They didn't know about college. They didn't know about the university.[43] They didn't go east of Park Avenue. They just didn't do it. It was common in those days that you knew your surroundings and you just kept within it. It was very segregated from that standpoint. Economically.

Before the next speaker began, Gabi had a question: "What did he mean, not going east of Park Avenue?"

I explained that in Tucson's early years, most Mexican Americans lived on the west side. A sort of a mental barrier existed between the "white" east side and the "Mexican" west side. Some drew that line at Stone Avenue, which ran through downtown. Others, including Frank's parents, drew the line at Park. The university's main gate is on Park Avenue, and the school spreads east from there.

Gabriela nodded. "Like a line in the sand."

"Exactly."

Rafael Gallego, 1986

My dad instilled in me really early in life to be a good and hard worker. In our culture that's done. The man works and the woman stays home and takes care of the house. That was definitely instilled in me. A good work ethic.

I was a good student. But let me give you an example of the attitude toward minorities. They assigned counselors to you. It was right before I was going in as a freshman. This counselor assigned me to wood shop, auto mechanics, and those types of classes.[44] Not knowing any better and saying, "I have no interest in auto mechanics," I just went with the flow. This was 1974, 1973. I ended up in a pretrade track rather than precollege.

The idea of college didn't really come seriously into my mind until seven years after high school. I didn't think I could cut it in college. I considered college a place where only the brightest of the bright go. I don't remember a lot of my Hispanic friends going to college.

I went to Pima[45] for one semester and didn't even finish that. I was working at a department store. My perception was, "Why do you go to college? To earn a decent living." At the time I was making pretty decent money for a single man, so I thought I just saved myself four years of grief. I worked there for a while. I met my wife and got married when I was nineteen years old.

I got another job opportunity in furniture sales and was making a fair living. I didn't like it. I got a job selling life insurance. For the first time ever I got to work in a shirt and tie. I was in an office building and had my own desk. Wow, I've arrived. I remember thinking, "Jeez, I didn't even go to college. This is great."

That was a disaster. It broke me financially and emotionally. Finally I said to myself, "I'm ready to work with my hands." So I went to work at the mine.

My dad retired from the mine. He put in thirty years at San Manuel, Magma Copper Company. I went over there and got a job. I was making $10 an hour. This was 1980. Good money. Great money. By that time we had a baby.

I remember thinking, "This is the ultimate." Being the sole breadwinner. Being able to support the family. $20,000 a year. My wife doesn't have to work. Those macho things came into my mind. Although I hated the job, it was great money.

We worked all three shifts, and I was breaking rocks. It was a dirty job. It was underground. It was dangerous. I started thinking, "Am I going to be like my dad? Spend thirty years here?" On the Fourth of July, 1982, I got laid off.

Got odd jobs here and there. Then I got a job at Hughes Aircraft in January of 1983 as a janitor. It was the only thing I could find. Most of the other janitors were also Hispanic. I would see people either my age or younger working on the assembly lines. I wanted to do that. So I started applying for different jobs, transfers or promotions.

I lost about three or four different job opportunities that I probably could have done, but they gave them to a brother-in-law's cousin or a brother-in-law or an uncle.

The last one I lost was a blessing in disguise because that was a true qualifications loss. The guy that got the job had an associate's degree from Pima College, something I did not have. That I could handle. But I also realized, "I'm going to be doing this forever if I don't go back to school."

I remember that day vividly. I was working swing shift, and I was at an all-time low. I said, "I got to go to school." The next day I went to the U of A and talked to Manuel Escamilla. For the first time in my life I was told not only that I could do it, but I will do it. And he said, "We will provide you with the guidance and whatever you need to do it."

I went from the gutter to walking about four feet off the ground. I applied and I started full time in January of 1984.

I remember getting the letter saying I was admitted to the university. I still have it. That's how I decided to tell my parents. I wanted to show them the letter. Here I am, a grown man, married and a father of two by then, and still seeking their approval. My dad was tickled pink. It was great.

When I left Hughes, I was making minimum wage. I remember at that time, because our son was just a baby and my wife was only semiskilled, it would have put us in the hole for us to find a sitter so she stayed home. I remember having public assistance help us out. We could not go any lower. Then Dr. Escamilla told us that I could apply for financial aid and get some grants. There was a light at the end of the tunnel.

Before we were in dire straits financially, but we couldn't see getting out of it. Now, with school, financially we were doing the same, but we were just a lot happier. We had a goal.

The day had grown old, and we could hear the boom of thunderstorms building outside. Interstate 19 between Tucson and Nogales is no place to be in a hard rain. Richard and Gabriela had several more errands to run before taking on the drive home. It was time to quit. Gabriela was charged up.

"You've really got me going," she said. "Now I'm dying to know how these stories turned out. Did they all graduate? Did they have to work to get through? They must've found it hard to have time for friends and just hanging out."

"Maybe we can talk next time you're up. If you're interested, we can hear a little more."

Gabriela and Richard stood, and we had another round of handshakes.

"Mr. Rochlin, thanks for taking all this time to talk to me," said Gabriela.

"Listen, it's really okay if you call me Jay. It makes me feel like an old guy when people call me Mr. Rochlin."

"Okay, Jay. And you can call me Gabi."

"Deal. Hey, maybe next time you're up I can show you around campus. I can tell we have lots more to talk about."

I watched them go. I felt a little better about what I'd undertaken, but it was still daunting to think that a teenager was hanging a big life decision on what I was telling her. And I thought maybe I was kidding myself. Maybe these stories of different lives lived in a different time were too much for a kid from Nogales, and she'd get home and decide her department store job was just fine. I remember being a seventeen-year-old kid from Nogales, looking up at the outside world and wondering if I had a place in it.

The rain started. It blew against my office window. I put my feet up and watched it. I really hoped I'd see Gabi again.

3 <

Social Class & the University

Not counting magazines, I generally have about two inches worth of mail waiting for me by ten o'clock every morning. Bulk mail usually lands in the trash before I land in the chair. Campus memos? I ignore them later. I cull out the personal letters first. Those I read. My eye caught a hand-addressed envelope with a Nogales return. It'd been just over a week since my visit with Gabi and Richard. I opened the letter.

> Dear Mr. Rochlin (Jay),
>
> Thank you very much for the time you spent with me. I'm sorry it has taken me so long to send you a thank-you note, but I've had a lot to think about since then. I have so many things to tell you. I hope you don't mind.
>
> I really hadn't spent a lot of time thinking about race in the way we talked about it. For most of us in Nogales, the black-white thing isn't really big. We spend more time worrying about money. I have a friend whose

*mom is a maid. She just laughs and says she doesn't care
who wears the shirt after she irons it as long as they pay her
a dollar to do it.*

*One thing I noticed was how focused some of the
people you told me about were. They knew college would be
tough, but it didn't seem to matter. They were just going to do
it, like some of the people you told me about who said it was
a given.*

*I'm worried because I'm not that sure. It really isn't a
given for me. I'm not sure I really belong there, or at any
college. I could do the school work, but it really doesn't seem
like a world that I belong to.*

Gabi ended by asking if she could visit me again. She was going
to be in Tucson a week from Thursday for a dental appointment. She
wanted to talk about making friends in college and just "fitting in."[1]
She left her home number and asked me to call to let her know. My
schedule was clear. And if it wasn't, I'd have cleared it. I was fond of
Gabi and her dad. I scribbled a note in my calendar to call her that
night. Then I read her letter again.

The crack about the maid and the shirt got me. I chuckled over
it a second time and glanced at a journal article on my desk. It was
about social class and educational attainment. I couldn't help but
shake my head and smile.

Is it race or is it class? The question had been an underlying
theme from the start of my study.[2] A lot of recent writing about why
minorities weren't proportionately represented in higher education
suggested that poverty, not race, was the reason.[3] But I wasn't sure
about the class theory. Race was the primary factor in shaping the
university experiences of those I interviewed. Even so, their ability to
achieve at levels higher than their early peers couldn't be explained
by any single factor. Grand theories are fine. But individuals, it
seems, are more complex, and for many, social class did matter.

In reading over their narratives, I was surprised to learn that
many parents and grandparents of my informants had been a part of

the Mexican elite prior to that country's revolution. Pancho Villa turned their lives upside down. His soldiers slaughtered them,[4] burned their homes, and stole their land. Many of these elites escaped to the United States, often with nothing but the clothes they wore. Some found their way to Tucson.

Even though they had little money, held menial jobs, or struggled as small-business owners, they remembered their roots. Class status was not something that a mere revolution could erase. These elites felt it was a matter of time until their families regained the trappings of their true social class. In many cases, it took only a generation. Many of their children and grandchildren became successful students at the University of Arizona between the 1920s and the middle 1950s.

Three individuals told particularly dramatic family stories—John Huerta, his sister Martha, and Arnold Elias, Martha's husband. John graduated in 1955. Martha entered college in 1952 as a music major and should have graduated in 1956 or 1957. But she chose to leave school to help Arnold complete his studies and start their family. Arnold graduated in 1959.

Arnold's grandfather was a *rurale,* an appointed member of the law enforcement establishment. On the eve of Mexico's revolution, a landed *rurale* was considered part of President Diaz's[5] element, and therefore marked for death by the rebels. Elias's grandfather sent his family across the border hoping to join them later. Arnold, sitting at a large executive desk, recalled:

> My grandfather was picked up in Agua Prieta as he followed his family. They were going to put him to the wall.[6] But one of his cousins, a fellow by the name of Puntao Colias Calles, happened to come into Agua Prieta while he was in jail.
> According to custom, when people like the revolutionaries came into town, one of the first things the leadership would do was go to the jails to find out who was in there, to see if there were any relatives in jail. He found his cousin Manuel and said to him, "I'm going to let you out and you get across that border because I cannot vouch for you after that." It was pretty close.

Elias's grandfather married a woman who'd also migrated north. They settled in Douglas, Arizona, in the 1930s, determined to rebuild their lives. They ran a dairy business. Arnold, the grandson, went on to become Tucson's postmaster and head of the U.S. Postal Service's southwest region.

Arnold's wife, Martha Elias, and her brother, John Huerta, trace their family back to two specific incidents during the Mexican Revolution.

In 1913, as Villa's army swept through central Mexico,[7] they stopped briefly in the city of Durango. General Villa sent word that he needed a horse trainer to take charge of his horses. The best trainer in the region was John and Martha's grandfather, Felipe Huerta, a stagecoach driver who lived in Durango with his wife and three sons. Several of Villa's men showed up at Felipe's home late one afternoon and ordered him to meet the General. As Felipe was led away, his oldest son, thirteen-year-old Refugio, nicknamed Cuco, tagged along.

Cuco watched Villa as he sat between two aides in a courtyard. The general was protected by armed soldiers. As he stood behind the soldiers, Cuco saw his nervous father, sombrero in hand, shaking on his feet before the general, answering questions with a simple, "*Sí, mi General. Sí, mi General.*"

I wondered if a high school senior would be moved by this kind of story? What in the world does a chance encounter between a Mexican revolutionary and John and Martha's grandfather nearly a century ago have to do with whether or not Gabriela Valenzuela might give college a try? I set aside her letter and slid my chair over to where I kept my interview transcripts. I found the white notebook and turned to John Huerta's section.

As I read, I could hear John's gentle voice recalling his father's story:

My father remembered Villa's voice as loud and intimidating. "Are you the Felipe Huerta who is the expert with horses?"

"Are you ready to travel with me and take care of my horses?"

"What about my officers, can you take care of their horses as well?"

Villa ended the brief discussion with instructions for Felipe to show up the following morning ready to travel. On the way home Cuco was so excited he could hardly contain himself. He was convinced that Felipe would certainly allow him to join this adventure with the great Villa.[8] Felipe quickly quashed his dream by sternly telling Cuco that neither of them would travel with Pancho Villa.

"But they will kill you if you don't obey," pleaded Cuco.

Felipe turned to him. "Tonight, we are leaving for the United States."

Abandoning his wife and family, Felipe and Cuco left under cover of darkness on a 500-mile walk from Durango to El Paso, Texas. In later years, Cuco described the ravages of war as seen through the eyes of a thirteen-year-old. He recalled the exhaustion, thirst, and hunger. They scavenged everywhere for food. Drinking water was almost impossible to find because wells and irrigation ditches were contaminated with dead cats and dogs.

Bodies hung everywhere, from telephone poles, trees. The stench of death was something he never forgot.

Four years later, in 1917, Mexican federal troops rode into the city of Monterrey and commandeered as their headquarters the poshest home they could find. It belonged to the López family. The parents resisted. Eleven-year-old Juanita López, the second oldest of four siblings, watched as the troops executed her parents.

In the panic that followed, the surviving children lost track of their younger brother Julian and never saw him again. The history from there is unclear. Martha said another brother went off to war and was never seen again. John believed that Juanita and two brothers made their way to Torreón, Coahuila, as orphans.

Juanita worked as a maid. At nineteen she fell in love with a man from America. He'd been working sixteen-hour days at a foundry in Los Angeles and returned to Mexico to find a wife. He entered through El Paso, where several years earlier, he and his father had entered the United States. Cuco Huerta and Juanita returned to El Paso, married, and the American Huerta family started in 1925.

I turned to the section where Martha was discussing the same story and read her words:

> They came to Tucson when I was two months old, and my dad worked for the railroad.[9] John is two years older than I am. He was born here. Then we went back to El Paso. I was born, and we came back. The rest of the family was born here.
>
> My parents were quite poor. We were a very large family. There were initially nine of us. My oldest sister and another brother died when they were quite young.
>
> My mother and my dad just felt that they couldn't support us just on that one salary, so my mother opened up a little grocery store. She used to run the store during the day with my older brothers and sisters. My dad would come from being a boilermaker, and he would cut meat all night. He was a butcher, so he would have the meat supply for the next day.
>
> My mother worked all day long and then she would sew. There were five girls in the family, so she would sew for us at night. And of course, my older sister was like my second mother, and she more or less took charge also. She and my mother raised us.

Juanita Huerta personified the hope of that generation of Mexican Americans. John Huerta remembers:

> Within a few months after our arrival, she had us building our own adobe home on the west side of Tucson. She made sure that the structure included living quarters at the rear and a large room in front to serve as a grocery store. Huerta's Grocery on the corner of Grande Avenue and Sonora Street opened for business in 1937 and literally became the first 7-11 store in Tucson. Those were the hours that the store was open.
>
> As the United States moved closer to World War II, business started to improve. When we went to war, the grocery store thrived as the only business in the St. Mary's Hospital area. In fact, we were so pressed that Dad left the Southern Pacific for several years to help out.

Most of the Mexican American people with whom I spoke, including John Huerta, were proud to claim their upper-class Mexican roots.[10] Another was G. A. Larriva from the class of 1929. "Father had mines and stores and properties," he declared. Like the Huertas, the Elias family, and thousands of others, the Larrivas left because Pancho Villa made it impossible to live in Mexico. The Larriva family entered United States territory on April 12, 1911.

Mary Ott, who graduated in 1935, remembers her Mexican mother as an *aristocrata* who never let the family forget. On the other hand, Mary says, her mother also realized that her former status didn't amount to much in Tucson. Because of that, her parents "were absolutely sure that the only way we would get anywhere" was through education.

Ed Ronstadt's father came to America because he was told it was "the land of opportunity" by his father. Richard Salvatierra's father studied music at the National Conservatory of Mexico at the beginning of the century. Robert Figueroa's father was a professor in Sonora and was a "gentleman farmer." Mario Yrún's mother was a teacher in Monterrey. Richard Pesqueira's mother was a school teacher and had been a tennis star at the University of Arizona in the 1920s.

The members of this group built their new lives in America through energy, hope, and entrepreneurship.

Mario Yrún, class of 1949, remembers his early family life:

> So you have a widow with three young kids, no means of liveli-hood, not knowing anyone. But my mother was a real self-reliant, self-sufficient person. She had been a teacher in Mexico.
>
> She opened a small grocery store at the corner of Convent and Simpson. There was a Chinese grocery store on the northwest corner and southwest corner. We had the northeast corner. The grocery store had two rooms and a cellar. We all grew up there.
>
> She never learned English and taught us how to read and write Spanish before we knew any English at all.
>
> Three boys and we worked. We all sold newspapers and magazines.

> We used to go to the Southern Pacific ice plant and get ice from the
> freight cars. We'd sell that and coal in the neighborhood. I started
> selling newspapers when I was six years old. I couldn't speak a word
> of English, but my brother used to put me on his bicycle and ride me
> to the El Presidio Hotel. I used to sit there with my newspapers.
> Couldn't speak English, but I knew how to make change. Papers were
> three cents at the time. I went from there to regular delivery at the
> newspaper.

Arnulfo Trejo's father opened a tiny store which eventually
became a combination store and a restaurant on Convent Street, 418
South Convent, corner of Convent and Kennedy. Arnold Elias's dad
opened a shoe repair shop nearby.

Richard Pesqueira spoke about being materially impoverished
but full of hope:

> We were poor. I'm telling you, we were poor, just as poor as
> people are now in that alley. We had our little piñata parties, and
> that was our one big thrill, and Christmas was one gift or two gifts.
> But there was never any doubt that my parents were thinking ahead,
> not day to day.
> We didn't have a car until I was twelve. But we were poor because
> of the Depression, not poor of spirit. The ambition was there. But I
> will be the first to say that we have too many stories of people today
> who have not been able to break through.

I kept wondering how Gabi would react to these stories. I didn't
see in her parents the same single-minded drive to succeed that was
so obvious in many of these stories. But she was tough, I had to give
her that. Maybe it was enough.

So were many of my informants. Even though most came from
poor families,[11] they held strong middle-class values. Over time they
moved into the ranks of the middle or upper-middle class. Successful
people. For them, the American Dream was no myth. It was their
lives. When I asked how they did it, I remember wishing their

answers were more complex. But they attributed their success to their parents' industriousness, their own education, hard work, and luck. They were unanimous that those values were important and deliberate parts of their upbringing as far back as they could remember.[12]

Even though they identified with the middle class, money was a daily concern for all but two of the African Americans I interviewed.[13] Their parents worked as domestics, janitors, or in other low-paying positions. Yet for Mildred McKee and Weldon Washington, to name two, at least one parent held a college degree, usually from a small, predominantly black college. They attributed their parents' underpaid, low-skilled jobs to racism. These parents, including those who lacked formal education, were well read and often spent a lot of time augmenting their children's education at home.

"My mother wasn't an educated woman," recalls Elgie Batteau. "She had to work, and she didn't have a chance. But education was a part of my rearing. They gave me every opportunity, piano lessons, violin lessons, and so on."

Elgie's parents worked on a ranch in Port O'Conner, Texas, on the Gulf of Mexico. There was only one school in the area. It was the 1920s, and neither blacks nor Hispanics were allowed to attend classes. The nearest black school was fifty miles away, a full day's travel in those days. Elgie's parents sent her there from third grade on.

"I was with my uncle and his wife and daughter," she says. "Once a month, it was arranged that either I would go down to see my parents or they would come up to see me. Getting my education, I had to be away from my mother."

Ernie McCray's mother graduated from Howard University, the prestigious African American university in Washington, D.C.:

> My mom worked for the telephone company for years. She was a
> college graduate and had a teaching degree, but she never used it.

She just started working for the telephone company doing menial kinds of things and later other duties.

We certainly weren't rich. But we were involved and turned on. My mother and I would travel every summer. My mother would save. We had this dinky little house. She put her money in vacations. We'd get on the bus or train. By the time I was fifteen, I had been in all the states except Florida, Georgia, and Alaska.

Olden Lee was the product of entrepreneurs. His mom was a cook and a cosmetologist. "I came from a group of self-help people," he said. He was taught not to rely on anyone but himself, a lesson he credits with much of his success.

Richard Davis's dad left home at twelve after completing sixth grade. He moved to Miami, Florida, from Fort Valley, Georgia, and took a job on a construction crew. He sent money home to his dad to help take care of the twelve-member family. He later married and had six children.

"Mother died when I was nine, so we were raised pretty much by our dad," said Richard. "He worked in construction until late in life when he became a janitor. He was a janitor of a school that my sister became principal at years later."

Lena Jones graduated with honors from Arizona in 1994. She remembers her grandparents being poor. Her father was in an orphanage for a while. Lena isn't sure why. "His mom felt that she didn't want to raise him and his eight or nine brothers and sisters," Lena said. "She just felt it was too much, I guess."

Both of her parents are high school graduates. Lena's mom has worked for the telephone company for thirty years. Her dad services master antenna systems for apartment complexes in New York City.

All of the parents and grandparents of my Mexican American informants began life in America with virtually no material wealth. They spoke little or no English, had limited formal education in the United States, and few professional role models. The common thread was that their parents had the utmost regard for education.

Diego Navarrette's recollections were not unusual:

> Dad went to tenth grade and stopped. I think it wasn't out of choosing. It wasn't that he didn't like school. It's that his parents had passed away, and since he was the youngest male of thirteen children, he became kind of like a waif, an orphan, and the older brothers and sisters would take care of him.
>
> Mother went to school during the Depression. Mother was born in 1916 so add fourteen, fifteen years to that, we're right around the 1930s, 1933, 1934. Mother did not finish high school but graduated correspondence school, the American Correspondence School out of Chicago.
>
> I remember that vividly because when we were living at 1443 South Tyndall, behind Elizabeth Borton School, which still exists, I would go to the mailbox and mail her lessons for her. She got her diploma through correspondence.

Tom Amparano's parents were in elementary school during the 1940s. His dad didn't make it much beyond sixth or seventh grade. "I think my mom went through ninth or tenth grade," he says. "She was a very bright lady. But the family was obviously too poor for her to continue. Then she worked. Once you could help the family out, you worked. There were very big families at the time and that was it."

Mike Duran, class of 1983, says his father "achieved a sixth-grade education and has been working since then, literally." His mother graduated from Tucson High School and worked for thirty-five years in banking.

For David Carranza, class of 1983, his dad was the high school graduate, but his mother "only went through the eighth grade."

Rafael Gallego, class of 1986, doesn't know if his mother ever went to school. "She probably has a third-grade education. My dad has about a fifth-grade education. But the school in Mexico does more in five years than most schools do here in twelve. My dad to this day can recite to you the different body parts he learned in third grade. He can name every bone still."

Gabi arrived at my office right on time. It was good to see her again. She smiled when she saw me and it just about took over the room. I could have flattered myself, thinking she was happy to see me. But more likely, she was glad to be out of the dentist's chair. Maybe it was a little of both.

She had on a red pullover, short sleeved, with a gold cross necklace. Her jeans were brand new, Levis. Her running shoes were Nikes, also red. The colors matched her red fingernail polish, standard for a Nogales teenager. Her dress was a little more informal than the first time, more relaxed. I took that as a good sign. She felt she could be herself.

Gabi jumped at my suggestion that we walk to the Student Union for coffee and cheesecake. I needed to keep up my fat intake. I had something else in mind, too, part of the campus I wanted Gabi to see. So off we went into postcard weather, one of those Arizona days that makes you think anything is possible. World peace. An end to hunger. A campus parking spot. We strolled along in silence.

The quiet was broken when Gabi set eyes on fraternity row. She let out a gasp, stared for a while, and said simply, "Wow!"

That summed it up nicely. It's impressive. The houses are grand and old, impeccably kept, majestic in a way. They have ivy-covered walls, putting-green lawns and colorful flower beds. With desert landscaping covering much of the rest of campus, fraternity row is like another world, and not just in physical appearance. Fraternities and sororities are a culture within a culture.

"Let's check out some of the houses," I said.

We passed the Kappa house. The Pi Phis live here. The Tri Delts, Kappa Sigs, SAEs.

"You know, Jay," Gabi said, "the more I see, the more I realize there's a lot about college life I don't know. I don't think I've ever seen the inside of a sorority house."

"Neither have I. Well, that's not true. Back during my last year of college I was in the lobby of the Jewish sorority once. I was meeting a date."

She looked at me curiously. "Jewish sorority? Why was there a Jewish sorority?"

"Back then Jewish girls weren't welcome in most sororities, so they formed their own."

"Gosh. Then there must've been Hispanic sororities, too?"

I cleared my throat. "Mexican American girls didn't join sororities, Gabi. First off, there were hardly any Mexican American girls going to school, and second, it cost a lot of money to be in a sorority."

"They look expensive. Are the rooms nice?" She stared up at the tall buildings. How mysterious they must've seemed to her. "What do you think about fraternities and sororities, Jay?"

Something popped into my mind, the memory of a game a colleague and I used to play. During rush week, Anna Marie and I would walk past fraternity row, usually on the way to a meeting or on some errand, and we'd challenge each other to find the first black or brown face in crowds of blondes, brunettes, and redheads. Lot of times neither of us won.

"Fraternities and sororities give a lot of kids a real sense of belonging," I said, then sucked in a deep breath. Did I really believe this, or was I just being a good soldier for my employer? I continued. "People who study these things say that if you find a place to really fit in, like a sorority, there's a better chance that you'll stick around and graduate.[14] For lots of kids, the Greek system is where they fit in. The living arrangements are great. You get a built-in set of friends and people to study with. And about three or four years ago, some students formed a Hispanic fraternity and two sororities."

No, I guess I believed it. Everyone needs a place. It was funny to be talking about this now. Just that week I'd re-read my research on what my interviewees thought about Greek life. They didn't paint a pretty picture. I thought back to my first meeting with Gabi, and how I'd bowled her over with too much negativity.

But enough time had passed since then. She was ready to hear the harsh message of my informants. It was clear and consistent over time that the very existence of Greek life was negative for them, beginning in the 1920s and continuing right up to the present.[15] But that question again: Was it race or was it class? My guess was both.

I wondered what Gabi thought. Fresh eyes might help me understand things better. I also thought it'd be good for Gabi to see that the Greek system, while not all bad, didn't offer a welcoming environment for the minorities I interviewed. I grabbed a stack of papers out of my shoulder bag.

"I've got something here you might find interesting," I said.

"More interviews I bet."

I handed them to her. "Take a look at these while we walk. I'll tell you if you're about to run into a tree. Or a frat boy."

The transcripts were arranged by decade. What astonished me about them was that neither the tone or the specific stories changed over half a century. She began reading:

G. A. Larriva, 1920s

> You didn't get asked to join a fraternity. The only reason I got asked was they were going national. One of the finest fraternities here needed my grades. I had very good grades so they asked me to join. I told them, sorry.

Nazario Gonzales, 1930s

> I would never attempt to join a fraternity. When I was in school, I wouldn't even try. I probably wouldn't have been accepted. I never tried the impossible. I didn't like the rejection. Yet my son was accepted into three. He wanted to be sure he was accepted. He took the third one.

Mary Ott, 1930s

I didn't think about joining a sorority. That was for the rich who didn't really know what to do with their money. I made friends with all kinds of people from all over. I did deliberately avoid sorority girls because they were stuck up.

Richard Salvatierra, 1940s

If you were an ethnic minority, you weren't going to be accepted into any fraternity. We all knew this, and those of us who were minorities also recognized that even if we wanted to and were accepted, we wouldn't have the money to do it. So we just cast it aside.

Laura Banks, 1940s

The idea of being in a white sorority was absolutely out of the question.

Mary Jo Yrún, 1940s

I do remember little tinges of envy when I was in my first year of college and had to help myself by working. This was the first time in my life that I met girls whose parents sent them to school and put them into sororities and do all that. I didn't even rush, but I never thought of not being a sorority person because of ethnic reasons. It was because of money.

Alfredo Márquez, 1940s

I joined a fraternity, Theta Chi. I don't remember if there were any other Hispanics in it. I wasn't very active in it. I knew some of the guys and they asked me to join. I didn't sense any discrimination there. I think there was some discrimination, particularly in sororities, probably some in fraternities, and some of the organizations. It's a fact of life.

Weldon Washington, 1950s

Phi Delta Kappa was a professional fraternity. It was an education fraternity. Phi Delta Kappa. That was the only one I was in. I was the first black admitted to it at the U of A, around 1953.

John Huerta, 1950s

We fully expected campus life to be dominated by the fraternities and sororities, yet it never entered my mind that I should join the Greek system. Money was an obstacle yes, but joining was never a priority. We had much more in common with the vets than with the frat boys. The Greeks drove fancy cars, dressed with smart slacks and short-sleeved shirts. We drove old cars, wore Levis, T-shirts, white socks, and penny loafers.

Martha Elias, 1950s

We were never asked into sororities, but you know what, I never expected it, so I never was really disappointed. I really didn't have time for it. I had to work in order to be able to go to school so I did. I didn't work too terribly long hours. I think I worked about three or four hours a night and that was it.

Ernie McCray, 1960s

I was in Kappa Alpha Psi, the black fraternity. We took part in something like a Greek Olympics, and you paired up with other groups. I remember having a white girl on my back in some kind of race, and some guys were having all kinds of trouble with that. Turning blue in the face and making comments.

Salomón Baldenegro, 1960s

I called them Greek assholes, and they would call me you greaser bastard, go back to Mexico. And I would say, "Fuck you, go back to . . . " The ROTC guys and the war guys and the peace guys would go at it. When I spoke about the grape boycott, the aggie fraternity guys were out there and man, we almost went to blows.

The only thing we had against the Greeks was that they were so goddamned elitist. They strutted around like they owned the university. And people still believe that. People still feel that way.

But the "spic" comments, the "go back to Mexico" comments, the "dumb Mexican" comments that I heard came during Speaker's Corner and during rallies. And we called them Greek assholes, and they were calling us dumb Mexicans. Fair game. The ROTC guys were calling the other guys sissies and cowards, and they were calling them warmongers. And so, those comments were there. And there was an occasional comment about interracial dating.

Frank Felix, 1970s

It was still a party school when I started. Fraternities and sororities were at their peak. We had no use for the Greek types. Screw
them. They were shallow at best. Bobbi asked me to a couple of her
functions. Right away, I got into fights. One of the fraternities, I
walked in and one of the members said, "What are you doing here?"

I said, "What the fuck, is it your business?"

"You're not a member."

"I'm here with a guest, and if you want to make something of it,
let's go outside and take care of it." And some guys came up to her
and said, "Bobbi, we think you better leave."

When they said that, I grabbed a guy and shoved him across the
room. He did a somersault. Made quite a ruckus as I was walking
out, but nobody did anything. I just figured, "OK, I'll walk out." I
expected to be hit on the head. Bobbi was upset. I said, "Bobbi, I
don't think this is going to work. I'm not part of your group. If you
want to go out together to other things, that's fine."

Richard Gonzales, 1970s

In the Greek system the attitudes stuck out like a sore thumb. You
could see that you were on the outs. You could walk into one of the
dances on a Friday or Saturday night at the university, and you could
see it from the dynamics in there what groups you were acceptable to
and which ones you were not.

You could go to the football games and go to the student section,
and there were sections where you knew that they were going to be a
little bit testier because you had all the Greeks sitting there.

I mean, we carved out our area for four years in Coffin Corner.
That was our area. My peer group, primarily Hispanics. We had also
Native Americans, Tohono O'odham.[16] We didn't need the Greeks.

And of course, then you have a group of five or six obviously
Hispanic types walking into sorority row. Nobody told us to get out of
there, but people would stop and look.

We reached the steps of the Kappa house. Gabriela was getting
a bit overwhelmed.

"Hang in there," I said. "I found some exceptions, too."

I told her about Richard Pesqueira, who went through the

university in the 1950s. For him, being a member of Sigma Chi was one of the most positive things that ever happened to him. He still identifies himself as a Sigma Chi. He saw himself as a "mainstream person." In high school he was a member of the National Honor Society and a baseball star. He saw himself as middle class. When he came to college, he went through fraternity rush. During college, he didn't have any Mexican American friends to speak of. He still wonders about that.

"I've always had to wrestle with this question, you know, who am I?" he told me. "In fact I remember giving a lecture in graduate school about the half-breed. The man without a country. The other end of the university pipeline was a white world, and you functioned in that world. You didn't get rewarded by being different. You got rewarded by being assimilated."[17]

Two Hispanic students walked by, laughing.

"A lot of minorities have made it through this school," I said. "Sure, they didn't have it as easy as some of the well-to-do white kids, but they had plenty of friends and lots of fun."

"But it sounds like it was awful unless you were part of that world. It was like minorities weren't part of the school at all."

"They weren't part of that social scene at all, no. But they created their own. That helped a lot of them stick it out. Feel like talking about it?"

"Sure," she said.

"Okay, first I'll give you some more bad news, and then the good news."

"Okay."

I explained that not only were the minorities I interviewed not part of the Greek system, they weren't connected to any other organized university activity either.[18] Blacks usually weren't welcome and they knew it. Hispanics generally participated more, but a lack of time and money got in the way. I remembered some of their comments.

"I didn't participate in extracurricular activities because I was working selling appliances," said Arnulfo Trejo, class of 1949. "That is one regret I do have."

Richard Gonzales, who attended the university in the 1970s, spoke from the same script. "I didn't participate in organized extracurricular activities in undergrad school," he said. "I was working almost full time."

Gabi was still holding the transcript papers. She flung her arms out at her sides as she walked. "Now you're really bumming me out. Thanks."

"But the good news is they didn't need Greek Life. They didn't need adult-supervised and -administered activities.[19] They were in college for an education. They got it. They left. Simple. Some of them made lifelong friends. But the point is, they connected and belonged to their own, self-made worlds."

It had surprised me to learn how my informants formed their own counter social groups. Not just cliques, but real clubs. They knew their status on campus—ignored, tolerated, or resented, depending on the day. And at times harassed. So they made their own way in a tough environment. I explained all that to Gabi and talked so long that she was laughing by the time I finished.

"What's so funny?"

"You, Jay. Something tells me we're going back in time again."

"Are you game?"

"Sure."

LAMBDA SIGMA ALPHA, 1920s

G. A. Larriva, about 1925, helped organize a Hispanic fraternity called Lambda Sigma Alpha. The Greek letters stood for "Latin Students of America."

"We had Argentineans, Venezuelans, and so on," he remembers. "And believe it or not, we had a couple of American boys.[20]

There was a fellow by the name of Kendall. He wanted to join us, so we let him join."

Why did G. A. and his friends start their own group? "We felt we were not considered for membership in others. Lambda Sigma Alpha had parties with picnics, but we did it for just having a place to live."

The group rented because they didn't have the money to buy a house as did the mainstream fraternities. "I became the president, and I would make those guys study," G. A. says.

CLUB LATINO, 1930s

During the 1930s, minority students often found their social connections off campus. Nazario Gonzales remembers Club Latino, which held dances on Sundays. And there was always the church. "The Catholic church was important because it was part of our social life," says Nazario. "The parades, the gatherings of families for fiestas. Lots of people. Lots of children. My grandfather would roast a pig."

Now and then an individual faculty member did care and made a personal difference. Nazario made one such connection during college. "Dr. Anita Post took a liking to me," he said. "She made me president of the Spanish Club. The Spanish club was where we started hearing about 'La Barca' and the plays and art. El Greco and Murillo and so on. The Spanish Club was important."

THE JOLLY JENSEN LASSIES/THE DAMIAN CLUB/
CÍRCULO ESTUDIANTIL, 1940s

"The one thing that I was very much aware of was to be active on campus, to run for office or to do anything like that meant that you had to belong to one of the organizations," says Anna Jolivet.

"There were none for black students. There were none that accepted black students. Even the Phrateres, which was a town girls' organization, did not take black women."

Jolivet did not look to the campus as a source for her social life. Neither did Laura Banks, who remembers being angry. "But they are not going to keep me from enjoying life." She and some friends formed a group called "The Jolly Jensen Lassies."

Laura and her mother owned a home on the outskirts of town. "The Jolly Jensen Lassies came out. It was like being in the country. We could be as loud and have as much fun as we wanted to. It was really important. We had a ball, but we had to generate our own fun."

The YWCA had an organization for black women, and there was the Ivy Leaf Club, a prerequisite to being in Alpha Kappa Alpha, a black sorority.

For some Mexican American students during the 1950s, their social lives remained in their original neighborhoods, centered around the church. Mario and Mary Jo Lemas Yrún, both college students at the time, met off campus at the Damian Club, a Catholic youth organization affiliated with All Saints Church.

"I wasn't aware of any formal campus organization for Mexicans," said Mary Jo. Unlike Anna Jolivet, Mary Jo was, however, a member of Phrateres, which apparently did accept Mexican American women.

Twenty years after G. A. Larriva helped organize Lambda Sigma Alpha, Arnulfo Trejo helped organize Círculo Estudiantil. That group's members were concerned about the lack of political participation by Mexican Americans. "Several of the Mexican American students in those days used to meet in front of the library. It was there we began to form that group. It was later called *El Foro*." Arnulfo adds, "It was a social group, too. It was a pretty nice group of about fifteen students."

"Hispanics were few and far between on campus," says John Huerta. He guesses there were fewer than 150 at any one time during his five years at the university. At that, he may have overestimated.

At one point in my research I examined old yearbooks looking for Hispanic or African American students. I searched for obvious Spanish surnames, then looked at all the pages of every yearbook between 1932 and 1959 in search of minority members. Even realizing that students weren't required to pose for pictures and that several minority students were in school during this period but not in the yearbook, I was surprised by how few I saw.

In 1932, there were photos of four minorities, and only two each for 1933 and 1934. In 1940, two; in 1941, none. In 1954, the year John Huerta remembers organizing the few Mexican Americans he could find, I found twenty-three Hispanics or African Americans in the university yearbook.

John's group was called Los Universitarios. The group held meetings, picnics, and eventually, fund-raising dinners. They raised enough money to award scholarships to younger college-bound Mexican Americans.

"It was never anything more than just a social organization," John remembers, "but it gave us a sense of belonging and helped to establish some lifelong relationships."

Elena Navarrette uses stronger words to describe what the group meant to her. "There was a club that really was a savior because it was a club of Mexican Americans, and that way, I was able to meet other Mexican Americans. Los Universitarios. I didn't know anybody. I didn't know anyone until I joined that club."

Diego Navarrette, Elena's husband, described Los Universitarios as a "social and a bonding as well as a survival group." The group, said Diego, was his "only port in the storm." He said, "It was the only place where you could seek some refuge. It was very important for me because I felt that I finally belonged to the university in some kind of tangible way."

During the time Diego was involved, Marty Cortez, a 1958 graduate, was president of Los Universitarios. She remembers a group of about thirty-five to forty people. She remembers helping to organize the group in 1956, during her junior year. The leaders hoped the group would bring Hispanic students into the greater university community. They also hoped to meet more Hispanic students and have a social outlet.

"We felt that we were an important part of the university even though not a whole lot of other people might think that," says Marty. "It did give us a sense of accomplishing something."

But it wasn't easy. "Father Curry wanted us to be associated with the Newman Club,"[21] Marty remembers, "and as a matter of fact, he got quite upset with us because we wouldn't come under the umbrella of the Newman Club. We wanted our club to be open to whoever wanted to join, not that you had to be Catholic. He was quite put out with us for a while."

Other students didn't necessarily share the need felt by John Huerta and Marty Cortez-Terrazas for affinity with Mexican American classmates. Richard Pesqueira wasn't even aware of the group's existence. "Figuratively speaking, I was on the other side of campus from a group such as Los Universitarios. Johnny Huerta, I knew him, although he was ahead of me. They were the more activist types already. I was not even aware that they existed as a group. Not at that time. I never related to it and never really knew much about it." Other students had questions. In Marty's words:

> When we started Los Universitarios, there were a lot of questions about "why" from the kids. They were afraid to identify with the group because they were trying to melt into the greater society. And to say they belonged to Los Universitarios? Why didn't we call it something else? Why did we have to pick a Mexican name? And was this for Spanish kids only? Some of the Mexican American kids asked if it was just for Spanish kids.

There was a lot of confusion, because for some kids, they didn't want to be openly a part of something to do with Mexican culture, and it was a little scary for some of them.

About four decades later Marty looks back at the group and wonders why she and her fellow Universitarios weren't tougher:

I think, why weren't we more militant? Why weren't we more active as far as demanding our rights? I think back on it now, and I think it was that we were so busy just trying to suffer through school. And we bought the package, we bought the propaganda to a large extent. We bought the whole kit-and-caboodle that minorities are "less" than the Anglo. We were in awe of the fact that we were just going to the university and making it, struggling through.

I think it was important for the group of us, too, because a lot of us were the first ones of our families to go to school. It was important that we do make it. It was kind of a pride and pressure at the same time.

1960s

The Civil Rights movement and the Vietnam War made Americans more aware of race and ethnicity. But relations on campus remained chilly. Richard Davis enrolled at the university forty years after Larriva formed Lambda Sigma Alpha. Richard and a close circle of friends formed a chapter of Alpha Phi Alpha, an African American fraternity.

"I think that when Alpha came along," Richard says, "we had some events, but those events were all African American events. They were not a part of the university. They were not part of the university because you didn't feel comfortable or like you could become a part of the university."

Richard, a 1969 graduate, now a lawyer, says, "I didn't get involved in a lot of activities like student council and so forth because, quite frankly, I never felt I was wanted."

1970s

Johnny Bowens came to the university as a graduate student and completed his master's degree in 1973. He was politically astute and academically prepared but didn't feel welcome as an individual.

"I wasn't involved with mainstream clubs," he says. "There was little in terms of my major. There was little socialization that was happening with students in my class. My feeling of connectiveness happened with students in the Black Student Union. There was a table, an African American table where, if you wanted to know what was happening during that week, or just a sense of coming in to get what I call refueled before you go back to your next class. It was in the cafeteria, main floor."

I'd talked a long time. Gabi was ready for coffee and cheese-cake. So ready she offered to buy. Of course I accepted. I work for the state. Gabi was impressed that I knew of a back-door basement entrance to the Student Union. We made our way to the Union Square, a little coffee bar. It wasn't hard to find. We followed the strong aroma of the beans. I wondered if the committee of state employees who dreamed this place up had ever set foot in a real coffee house.

I looked over the crowd. Young Republicans. Short hair. Eddie Bauer labels. Obsession cologne. Door-to-door salesman smiles. How would this group react to a Lawrence Ferlinghetti reading? Or a surprise appearance by Doc Watson?

"This is so cool," Gabi bubbled. "This is going to be my hang-out if I get to come here."

"Not if," I corrected. "When."

She liked the sound of that. Her grin stretched from ear to ear. She yanked a five-dollar bill from the pocket of her jeans and started toward the order line. But she turned, parked her hands on her hips, and curled her lips in thought.

"The thing is, I mean, forming your own clubs is cool, and I'm sure it helped. But it sounds like they missed out on stuff. All they did was go to class, hang out with friends just like themselves. And work."

Just like the white kids. That's what I thought. But I didn't say it.[22]

"It's not that simple," I said. "Nothing in this world is. Tell you what, I've got these other files of interviews that I haven't really studied yet. Lots of stuff in here." I fished through my bag. I found a bagel that looked like it dated to the second Nixon administration. I should call anthropology. "I labeled this file 'Friends and Dating.' Let's split it up and see if we can figure this out."

Gabi got the coffee and cheesecake. We pored through the files as we ate. It seemed like every experience was different. Gabi read aloud the words of Nazario Gonzales, who went to the university in the 1930s.

"My friends were mixed," Gonzales said. "Way back in fourth grade, there was a fellow named George Ramage. We were very, very close. Then there was Robert Burns. And Bill Mathews[23] was an everlasting friend until his death around 1988. I didn't date Anglo girls. I had a girl I loved very much, but I never dated her."

The first one I came across was Laura Banks. "My social life was not at the university at all," she said. "I had no best friends in terms of somebody who would come home with me and have dinner. Or exchange and spend a weekend. I didn't have that in college. I never dated a white guy. I only dated black fellows, but none of them were university students. When I think about it, at the university, I was always walking by myself, going to the library."

I remembered well my interview with Laura. She had tears in her eyes as she spoke those words. We read on.

Alfredo Márquez, 1940s

> My friends were Hispanics and Anglos. I had time for a social life. I dated both Anglo and Hispanic women. I had time for drinking beer and studying.

Mario Yrún, 1940s

> I was friends with a lot of the veterans, of course, and also people who worked at the newspaper same as I did. Most of them, about seventy percent, were Anglo. I met a lot of people in school. I could deal with people at the university and business people, and I could go down to the toughest barrio and get along, or go to the two dance halls on the west side. Never any problems. I dated during college. Mostly Anglos.

Arnulfo Trejo had a good mix of friends. "George Miller[24] was a good friend of mine," he said. "Jim Corbett[25] was also in our group. I dated both Anglos and *mexicanas*.[26] Not seeing other Mexican Americans on campus didn't bother me. It maybe was an advantage. I was the only one of a minority. I can recall that I had some of the better dates."

Hadie Redd, 1950s

> I didn't have much of a social life. No women. None at all. We had friends that were out in the city. I was fortunate though. I met a very lovely lady. She lived here, but was going to nursing school in Phoenix. I met her up there. She is now my wife, Theresa Redd. We're still together.

Some said that dating between minority women and Anglo men was sometimes awkward.[27]

Evelia Martínez, 1970s

> I took a sociology class in the evening and became real good friends with a guy who was a track star. He was white. I remember

him asking me out, and I just panicked. I kept turning him down until finally I told him I had a boyfriend, even though I didn't.

He was a neat person. He and I became good friends. We'd talk and he would wait for me after class. He would look for me. But I was just panicked. He lived at the dorm. He'd walk me to my car and make sure I got to my car okay. I didn't know how to handle it. I was still living at home, and I didn't know what my mother would say.

I hadn't dated much. I didn't start dating until I was in college. I went to the prom with my brother's best friend. He was like a brother. That was okay with my mom for me to go to the prom with him because she knew him. But I really had never dated until I got to college and even then, as a freshman, I dated very little.

I don't remember dating college guys, probably guys from the neighborhood because it was safe—whatever safe meant at that time. I started dating, but I was still dating Mexicans.

Robin Lemon, 1980s

I dated some white guys. And sometimes I felt like they had a hard time with it, more than I did because, you know, you get the stereotype of bringing a black girl home to meet mom. I think sometimes it wasn't as accepted.

I felt that during the times that I dated Anglo gentlemen, their families had a hard time with it. So I wouldn't pursue it, and I didn't want to be in a situation where anyone had to hide me. In instances like that, I would become angry because I would look at the two families, not that I think this way, the credentials of the African American family was a lot higher than the Anglo, and you still have the nerve to be prejudiced. Well, okay, then let's let it go. That's usually what would happen.

We came to some examples of married students. For them, college social life didn't have much to do with whether they graduated or not.[28] As for women, we couldn't figure out whether being married was good news or not. In reading the transcripts, Gabi noticed right away that a lot of them quit school to support their husbands, especially in the 1940s and 1950s.

She found my interview with Mary Jo Yrún, who should have graduated in 1946. Even though she was ahead of husband Mario, she was the one who left college to support his education. "It was my decision," Mary Jo said, "and all I can think of is I knew I had to save money to get married. In those days there was no question. Mario had to finish school."

Martha and Arnold Elias married during her third year of college. She should have graduated in 1957. Only one of them could afford to be in college at any one time, so it was Martha who left.

"I was ahead of him," she admits, "but you have to remember that in my culture, it was more important that he be the bread-winner.[29] That was the way I was raised, and I think it was a good decision. We discussed it, and it was easier for me to say that I would stay and work and you go to school."

Elena Navarrette, in school about the same time, says she decided on her own to have a baby and stay home.

Even though being married didn't help women get through college, most of my informants said it was a decision couples made together. And because they were poor, it had to be one or the other. That meant, of course, that the men ended up with degrees and careers and the women didn't.[30] But the men worked hard and appreciated what their wives did for them, and to some extent, that motivated them to make it through.

We read some more. I found my interview with Arnold Elias. He had to work two or three hours every night and all day Saturday and Sunday. Half a generation later, Tom Amparano and his wife decided that he'd be the one to pursue a degree. He remembers that the turkey was always cold at Thanksgiving because papers were always due about that time. He spent one Thanksgiving day at the library.

Mike Duran, who graduated in 1983, tells a very different story:

> My wife and I were sitting in my little blue Toyota pickup in the driveway of our first apartment after we had gotten married. I had picked her up from work. I had my soiled jeans on, my soiled tee shirt on, and I was sweaty from my Mountain Bell lineman job. The

night before, we had looked at my transcript and talked about it. My wife had gone to school a semester or two, so she really didn't have any units to speak of. We sat there in the truck after we pulled in the driveway at home and said, "Well, let's make a decision. Who should go?"

I said, "I've got the good job, the benefits. Your job's okay. You don't really like it there." She looked at me and said, "But you've got more units and you're going to finish faster. And you're going to get out there and make twice as much money faster than I will." So the decision was made then for me to go.

My wife was working full time. Being a Hispanic male, I certainly had to swallow a lot of pride having my wife put me through school.[31] So I wanted to demonstrate to her and the rest of my family that this was not going to be an unusual situation, even though it was unusual in and of itself. I was still going to have a family life to try to balance school, even though I was working very hard at school. After I finished law school, my wife was able to quit Southwest Gas and go to school and have a baby. She's now in graduate school at the U of A.

It seemed that barriers were the theme of every transcript Gabi and I read. What varied was how each of the speakers overcame them. Ernie McCray said that even though he "knew all the black folks" on campus, fewer than fifty,[32] he mainly "hung around with childhood buddies."

Diego Navarrette, also a 1960 graduate, was an English major and had many friends in the department. "We studied together. We'd go to each other's houses. But I couldn't feel at home. It was too superficial."

Carlos Vélez-Ibáñez, class of 1961, remembers socializing and dating only other Mexican Americans:

Mexicans from my neighborhood. Mexicans from the university. As far as Anglo girls, they wouldn't look at us. I never dated them. Me and my friends did not fit with non-Mexicans.[33]

The only group of non-Mexicans in my world were Anglos who became highly Mexicanized. These were people who were taking courses in Latin American history and some of the same courses I was taking. Some of these people, who were very bright and smart, also had a cultural affinity for the language and for the population. So they would hang out with us.

Six of the African Americans I interviewed attended the university on athletic scholarships. They found community among teammates.

Olden Lee, class of 1968, credits his teammates with encouraging him to stay in school. He remembers football being all-encompassing, leaving little time for anything but studying. "My friends were athletes, not the general students," he says. "I think, quite candidly, that some of the guys on the coaching staff had some pretty serious biases. But the athletes themselves were a great group of guys."

Robin Lemon echoes that. "Most of my friends were athletes because you were over there at McKale[34] practicing. I wasn't lonely on campus. But there is a distinction between athletes versus non-athletes. You have an immediate camaraderie with the athletes."[35]

For some students, though, the university opened up entire worlds of friends and ideas. Willie Cocio played and sang folk music as a university student in the early 1960s.

> I had no barriers. I think being an entertainer opened a lot of doors for me. We were actually kind of popular. We were sought for concerts. I had friends from Africa, from Mexico. There was one guy from North Vietnam, from Hanoi, at the U of A. Everybody called him Foo. So there was a real cross section.
>
> My singing partner was a towhead with blue eyes, so we were like salt and pepper, and I sang blues with him, and all of his people said, "Wow, this guy can sing blues." And show tunes and folk songs. And he sang in Spanish, and so we harmonized in Spanish, and he had a good accent.

Julieta Gonzalez, class of 1973, a flute player in the marching band, knew many students from Mexico and other countries. She also drank coffee with graduate teaching assistants in the Student Union and formed friendships with professors.

At the other end of the spectrum was Salomón Baldenegro. He arrived on campus during the late 1960s and, true to the times, was ethnically aware and political.

"When I came to the university, I experienced one of the biggest cultural shocks of my life,[36] he says. "Damn. When I got here there was, I found out two years later, 125 Hispanic-surnamed people at the university.[37] But that included the Mexicans from Mexico and Latinos from South America. So there must have been about sixty Chicanos, Mexican Americans. But the nature of the Chicanos who were here was very different."[38]

Not only did Sal feel alienated from the mainstream university, but he also felt a class gulf between himself and most of his fellow Mexican Americans.

I don't mean this as a condemnation, because they are good people, they were just different. They were eastside Mexicans[39] most of them. My sense was that most of the Chicano kids that were here were Salpointe[40] graduates. Very few of us were from Pueblo,[41] Tucson High,[42] working-class guys. There were some, but very few.

I wound up my first couple of years socializing more and made some of my best friendships with the gardeners. They would eat on the bottom part of Old Main, that little porch out there, and I'd go eat with them and I would talk to them. In fact, four of the guys couldn't speak English at all. When I organized the literacy project, some students went down and taught them English. And we would visit and talk. I tried to organize them into a union during my junior year of university. We lost by one vote. We almost had one. But the first couple years were a culture shock.

Other students consciously considered the on-campus options for social life and rejected them. For Jim Garcia, class of 1975, the reason was time:

I didn't belong to any of the organizations here on campus. I didn't join MEChA.[43] I may have jumped into one meeting one time and said, I don't want to do that. I was too busy working. I was too busy doing other things and improving my own personal skills that I didn't want to bother with that.

Most of the friends that I had in the work environment and otherwise were Anglo. There wasn't a ton of Hispanics going to the university. There was a few from Pueblo,[44] and some were from Tucson High. They were all in a little nucleus at New Start.[45] That's where you saw all the browns. You go anywhere else you didn't see anybody. I didn't have time to get involved in school other than classes at all. I did help, off and on, with incoming kids at New Start.[46] That was it.

Gabi and I came to my interview with David Carranza, class of 1983. She read it and handed it to me, and I read it again. It synthesized a lot of the issues we'd been hearing about.

I really was kind of separated from the school because I had one goal in mind—graduating. I made a lot of friends. I knew I was different, but I had a lot of white friends. I still had my Mexican friends. The way I got to have all these friends was that I would invite them to my mom and dad's all the time. That made a difference. My friends got to learn a little bit more about us.

The thing that I always tell the white folks is you have more to learn about me than I have to learn about you. So that's what I did. In fact, when I was going back to junior college, we had the entire baseball team eat in my house. We had steaks, tortillas, frijoles. The guys were saying, "Wow!"

I needed my Mexican friends. I drew from them. When I was in school, all the groups that they have now were just forming—MEChA, for example, was founded in 1969 and has been in continuous existence since then.

We used to hang out and talk about what was going on in school. We would talk about how teachers handled people differently. Issues on race concerned us. I kind of looked beyond that. I knew I was going to get through and get out and become successful. I didn't want to dwell on things that would hold me back.

I didn't have enough time to get involved in different groups. I was working as a salesperson and I was traveling to Mexico. I lived in an apartment. I was somewhat removed from the university. I dated mainly Hispanic girls. They were friends from high school. I didn't think at all about fraternities. Rushing, being pledged, and all that stuff. Me, I wanted to make sure I graduated from this institution.

It was time to meet Gabi's mom back at the office. We started to leave the coffee bar. At the door Gabi looked back and stared for several seconds. If I had to guess, I'd say she learned something in there. I know I did.

On the way back to my office, Gabi mentioned something she'd noticed—how common it was that the people I interviewed worked their way through college. In fact, it was an integral part of their experience.[47] She found nothing especially burdensome about that. She worked hard at Capin's Department Store. Her dad worked hard and so did her mom at home. It was normal. It was life. And in some ways, her tone suggested, it was good.

"Work isn't a big deal to me," she said. "If I come to school here, I'll work. For sure. I'd work if I stayed in Nogales, too."

"True, but . . ."

She was excited to be taking up the issue and kept on. "Don't a lot of kids work during college? White kids as well as Hispanics and African Americans.[48] Am I missing something?"

"Probably. Look at it this way. Is it fair that some people work forty hours a week while others don't but still have to compete for grades as if the playing field were equal?"

"Well. I don't know." She shrugged. "Some people are tall and some are short."

"Come on, Gabi. You can't compare the two."

"Some are smarter, too. Some girls at my school don't even have to study. They can ace tests like crazy."

"But some don't even have the chance to study because they're spending forty hours a week cleaning floors, bagging groceries, and flipping burgers or whatever."[49]

Gabi shook her head. "I just don't agree with that, but I can't explain why."

"Sure you can." I wanted to draw her out. I liked that she wasn't accepting everything put in front of her. She was trying ideas on for size and throwing off the ones she didn't like. With pretty good arguments, too. College material for sure. But did she know that?

"I just can't see how working through college is bad, that's all. It's just part of how we live. I don't want to be one of the rich girls, curlers in my hair, getting handed everything." Gabi kind of laughed. "I wouldn't know what to do with it anyway."

We'd stumbled onto one of the liveliest debates surrounding the question of class and opportunity—whether students forced to work during college were victims, too, just like those targeted by discrimination or bigotry. I thought Gabi was being naive. But I admired her for sticking to her position.

"Why should I complain and feel like a victim?" Gabi said. "Because I might have to work for something I want?"[50]

Some of my informants might agree. Mario Yrún started working selling newspapers when he was six. He couldn't speak English, but he could still make change. He worked for the newspaper through high school, from midnight to seven in the morning in the circulation department. His physics and English teachers were understanding when he fell asleep in class, the first two of the morning. Even though he didn't do well in high school, he credits a good amount of his success later in life to his exposure to new worlds as a result of work.

Richard Salvatierra said that working to help the family was always part of his routine. "That's how it's always been in my family," he said. "We've all had to pitch in with work around the house, and when we could, with money."

Salvatierra had to work several hours a night, and as a result, he was only an average student. But he worked at *The Arizona Daily Star*. He also worked at the university's news office. The way he tells it, working was part of his education.

Same with Laura Banks. She lived at home but still needed to work.[51] African American women couldn't get hired at department stores or drug stores, so she spent Saturdays ironing and cleaning in private homes. One of her employers was Richard Harvill,[52] at the time a university economics professor. Harvill and his wife befriended her and were a source of much encouragement. That continued after Harvill became university president.

In no way did Banks and Salvatierra fit the stereotypes often attached to their races, such as the "lazy Mexican" or "shiftless black." Nothing could be more blatantly false, unfair, and wrong.[53] Gabi and I agreed on that without question and wondered how anyone could listen to or read the stories of the people I interviewed and consider them lazy.

Anna Jolivet, 1950s

I would go to school early in the morning, go to my job in the midday, go home, wash, start dinner, and go back to school in the evening. Whatever had to be done. You planned and scheduled your day so you took care of everything.

Salomón Baldenegro, 1960s

My freshman year here was a really bad one. Not bad, it was rough. I lived with my grandmother, and she was disabled. So it was just she and I. I would wake up in the morning, and I would feed her. I would dress her because she couldn't move too well. I'd give her her medicine. And I'd come to school.

About ten thirty or eleven, I would have to be back around eleven, and I didn't have a car so I would have to walk or take the bus, and I'd have to go back about eleven, feed her again, and many times, help her to the bathroom because she couldn't get there. She could barely walk. And then come back to class and then go back home. It was real rough in that sense.

I didn't mind it because my grandmother and I had a great relationship. I muttered sometimes because it cut into my social life a lot. But I didn't really begrudge it because my Nana and I were just super close. But it did cut into my social life, and it made it really hard. Between classes I couldn't go to the library and study. I was working work study, about fifteen hours a week, at Ag-Biochem.

Willie Cocio, 1960s

> I did everything from ceramic work to foundry work to construction work to carpentry, building houses, worked TV. Just wherever I could get the job.
>
> Some teachers felt I didn't have the commitment to school because I didn't have twenty-four hours a day to devote to their particular class. I said, "To me commitment is showing up at this point. I just worked eight hours in an iron foundry."
>
> When I got married, I had up to three jobs during school. At 7 in the morning I'd be at KGUN-TV till 2:30 P.M. Then at 2:30 P.M., I'd go to a sandal shop and work till around 6:00 P.M., and then I would either go to classes, or on the days I didn't have classes, I would entertain. There are no saguaro thorns in my back.

At times the pressure was intense. Arnold Elias came close to quitting. He was working at a grocery store when he was offered a job as a manager with a starting salary of more than $300 a month. To Arnold, after trying to survive and pay the bills on less than half that, it seemed like a fortune. Arnold went home and told Martha about the opportunity:

"I was so pleased with myself because of the offer," he remembers. "So I went home that evening after school and after going to work, and said to Martha, 'God, I think I'll drop out of school and take this job. This is a tremendous opportunity.' She looked at me and I'm glad she didn't have a pan in her hand because she probably would have creamed me with it. She said, 'Hey, we've worked too long and too hard to quit at this point. We're going to go through, and we're going to finish this thing, and we're going to do what we need to do.'"

Arnold said he was tired of working and going to school and studying and not having a social life and not having weekends with his wife. But, he says, good sense prevailed. Arnold listened to his wife and, in his words, "That decision changed a whole career path. It was really hers."

Evelia Martínez did quit. She left the university two classes short of graduation. She was doing well in school and had even been offered a scholarship to law school in Indiana. But she left anyway.

"It was a financial decision," she says. "I got offered a full-time job. I couldn't afford to continue. I needed to start working. Looking back, it was the wrong decision, but I had nobody to guide me, to say, 'Evelia, you really need to finish.' Or, 'Evelia, you're this close. Just stick it out another semester or summer school.' The lack of a degree has always haunted me all my adult life."

Rick Gonzales worked between thirty and forty hours a week during college, first at a convenience store. Then he added a job in the public defender's office for prelaw students.

"Other students who didn't have to work didn't bother me," he says. "No, actually, I didn't even think about it. We'd toss that out, though, as an argument in law school. We were sitting there explaining lower GPAs and affirmative action, and I thought, 'Wait a minute, if I had had a free ride with dad paying my trip, I would have had great grades, too. Let's see what your grades would look like working thirty to forty hours a week.'"[54]

We were almost at my office. We saw Gabi's mom waiting on the steps. She waved and smiled. The smile was generous on her part because we were a half hour late. But our spirited debate had another round to play.

"Do you see what I'm saying, Gabi? How Rick Gonzales proves my point? He had a hard time competing with his well-off classmates because he had to work."

"Tell me what became of Mr. Gonzales? How did his life turn out?"

"It turned out great. He's a partner in a very successful law firm. Matter of fact, he ran for public office."

"Hmmmm."

"Hmmmm, what?"

"Doesn't that prove it can work out? You can't argue with results. He made it."

She'd set me up on that one. I stammered for a response, but it never passed my lips. I think I was going to say something about how the "system" had to allow some members of "the subordinate classes" to succeed.

"I hate to interrupt you scholars," said Gabi's mom. "But it's a long ride back to Nogales. *Vámonos.*"

4 <

Encounters with Racism

Gabriela's feeling ran deep. I already knew that. But I didn't know about her fiery temper. I got a taste of it during our third meeting. At my suggestion, she returned to campus for another visit. Student volunteers sometimes act as guides for high school seniors and their parents. One of the guides, Lisa Macaffee, works in my office. I arranged for Lisa and Gabi to tour campus together.

I was returning to my office that afternoon when I saw Gabi, already sitting at the table. Even though I first saw her from behind, I could tell something was wrong. The stiffness in her shoulders was plain. She turned when I called a cheery hello. The skin on her face was tightly drawn.

"Hi."

That was it. Hi. As if I needed more evidence that this had been a rotten day. I tossed my bag on the desk.

"Okay, let's hear it. Something happened."

"Nothing happened." She folded her arms across her chest.

I sat opposite her. "You talk, I listen."

"There's nothing to say."

I waited her out. It wasn't long before she spoke.

"You don't have any idea what it's like to be me," she blurted. "You're a guy, you're white. You always knew you'd go to college. You grew up in Nogales. Okay, great. But you can't even speak Spanish."

Gabi needed to unload, and for the moment, I was the target. Fine. I could've pointed out that in my day, students were routinely punished for speaking Spanish in class, and even on the playground. Even non-Mexicans, like me, were kept from speaking Spanish.

I gave her time to cool. She looked around the room, her eyes blazing. After a moment they filled with tears. She wiped her sleeve across her face and sniffed.

"Sorry. I'm really sorry."

"It's okay." I gave her another minute. "Tell me what happened."

"Maybe I'm just too sensitive. I'm not usually like this."

"Did someone say something to you?"

"Not exactly."

"Well?"

She ran her sleeve under her nose again and sucked in a deep breath.

"I was upstairs, okay, in the Student Union. Me and Lisa. After lunch, it was. She was showing me the student government offices, where the kids up there hang out. She wanted me to meet this girl, January Esquivel.[1] She's from Nogales. She's a student senator, and she might run for student body president."

"Yeah, I've heard the name."

"Okay, so there's these cubicles up there where the students have their computers and phones. Lisa and I are in there, and we're talking, and I hear some guy in the next cubicle talking to another guy about scoring with the new Mexican chick. And the other one goes, 'Oh, she's probably just some Mexican friend of January's from Nogales.' They were talking about me.

"It really got to me. I don't know why. I guess I was nervous being there in the first place. I don't think I've ever been called 'some Mexican.' And I hate the word 'chick.' And 'score.' I don't know, it's weird."

Listening to her, my mind drifted back. I remembered a mouthful of dust and an old pickup truck. I was nine. Six cub scouts, hanging on for dear life in the bed of Bob Mendez's pickup, bounced along the Ruby Road north of Nogales. It was our first overnighter. We had sore backs, dust in our eyes and hair, and stiff legs. It was a blast. We couldn't stop giggling.

Out of the blue, one of the boys put a finger against the tip of his nose and pushed down. The others laughed out loud, following his lead. And they were looking at me. I had no idea what the game was, so I didn't play.

That night as I roasted marshmallows at the campfire, Allie Connor parked at my side and said, "You're still my friend, Jay," and touched my shoulder. "It's not your fault you're Jewish."

Trouble was, no one had ever told me about Jewish noses.

Gabi stared at me. It was my turn to talk. I could tell she expected wisdom from me, but even on my best days, I don't have much of that. An ambulance screamed past out on Speedway, and even that shrill interruption didn't break her stare.

"So the guy was a jerk."

Sometimes I startle myself with insights like that. Gabi piped up again, saving me from having to say more.

"The thing is, I never thought of myself as different from anybody else. Down in Nogales, most of the kids in high school are Mexican American. We don't even think about it. My friend Sara's grandparents came from Romania. I don't think of her as a Gypsy. It's weird, these categories." She shook her head. "I wish I could get what that guy said out of my mind."

I thought back to my junior year at Nogales High. October 1966. I was president of the drama club and fancied myself a playwright. We traveled up to Tucson for an oral interpretation competition. It was at the university in the Speech building. The room was packed with teenagers who thought they were actors. At the back sat three adult judges. But my mind was on the Mexican American girl sitting near them. It was my turn. I was supposed to read from a play I'd written, but all of a sudden I got a case of the nerves. Some of the things I wrote were harsh, and I wondered if it would offend this girl. Should I skip the reading and forfeit the round?

Back then in Nogales, it seemed to me that all the teenage girls dated guys in their twenties from across the line. Mexico. To my sixteen-year-old heart, that was a grave injustice. So I sat down with my Smith-Corona 210 and pounded out a script that nailed both the guys from Mexico and their Nogales girlfriends.

Students, with their teachers, would pick out a three- to five-minute excerpt from some American classic, such as *Our Town* or *Bull in a China Shop.* Other students at the competition were reading from Beckett or Albee. But I was determined to read from Rochlin. Faculty advisor George Papçun had encouraged me. He was an ACLU activist.

When the judge called my name I stood on wobbly legs and made it to the front of the room. The only thing I saw in the crowd was the face of that girl. This wasn't a competition I was going to win. I knew that. But the purpose of art isn't to comfort, I told myself. I'd make my statement.

One of my characters spoke the epithet "dumb Mexican." I also uttered the word "spic." When she heard that the girl quit staring at me and lowered her eyes. I still wonder if she blew it off or if my words wounded her? I've thought about that for thirty years. But I still see her face. Maybe she still hears my words.

Would Gabi always hear the voice of that guy who wanted to "score" with the "Mexican chick"?

"Is this what the university's going to be like for me, Jay?"

"Some days, I'm afraid so."

"Will I have to stop being Gabi and become a Chicana? Or a Latina, or a Hispanic woman? Or a Mexican American female, or a woman of color, or a minority? Or is it going to be 'Mexican chick'?"

"It's funny. We've got diversity action committees, minority affairs deans, cultural centers, you name it. Some recommend theme dorms, ethnocentric majors, everything you can think of.[2] And some idiot's wisecrack has you thinking college might not be a good idea."

Gabi had done her homework, again. She brought up one of the books I'd recommended. It's called *Words That Wound*. It's a collection of essays by four of the leading critical race theorists. Gabi was particularly interested in a chapter by Mari Matsuda called "Public Response to Racist Speech." One of her points is that victims of racist speech often don't have the words to describe what they're feeling, or why they feel that way, and in frustration, sometimes blame themselves.

"I understand that now," she said. "Totally. There's a poem in that chapter. I have it here." She got a piece of paper out of her back pocket. "I wrote it down. I'm not sure I get it, but I wanted to remember it."

The title was a mouthful, "Poem for the Young White Man Who Asked Me How I, An Intelligent Well-Read Person Could Believe in the War Between Races." It was written by Lorna Dee Cervantes. Gabi read aloud the lines she'd written on the page:

> everywhere the crosses are burning,
> sharp-shooting goose-steppers around every corner,
> there are snipers in the schools . . .
> (I know you don't believe this.
> You think this is nothing
> but faddish exaggeration. But they
> are not shooting at you.)[3]

"That sounds pretty paranoid to me," she said. "But I guess they're not really shooting at me."

"Me either. But the people I interviewed were convinced the shooting's been going on for a long time, and probably still is."

"If I come to college, will I be shot at?" Gabi asked.

"I'm not optimistic."

I explained how nearly all the black students I spoke with had endured severe racism, and to a lesser extent, so did the Hispanics.

"You might not think of it this way, Gabi, but what you experienced today was racism. It's what Matsuda was writing about. And Derrick Bell and Patricia Williams and Richard Delgado."

"It's funny," she said. "I feel like I've gotten to know them. At least their ideas."

"What they say, basically, is that racism and discrimination are facts of life, almost starting points. Then they move on to how some people of color are subordinated by the dominant white society. Whites keep getting the perks. Minorities are stuck in the background."

"Did everyone you talked to say the same thing?"

"Well, on whether it was worth it, yeah. Everyone I talked to said it was worth it to get a college education."[4]

"But what about racism? Did everyone say the same stuff?"

"Only three said they experienced no racism. Mary Ott and Edward Ronstadt. They were in school in the 1930s. And Richard Pesqueira in the 1950s. They fit in with mainstream Anglo culture. They chose that. African Americans didn't have a choice."

She wanted to know what I meant, and I wanted to explain. We decided to talk about it over an early supper at Geronimoz, a restaurant on the west side of campus. The walk would do us good.

On the way out of my building, we noticed a group of Hispanics gathered around a conference table. They included John Huerta and Marty Cortez, two of the founders of Los Universitarios.

Huerta and Cortez, along with Arnold Elias and Evelia Martínez, founded Hispanic Alumni. They raise money to help Hispanic students attend the university.

I explained to Gabi that the meeting in progress was to plan an upcoming banquet. Gabi nodded and stared. She was putting faces to the names she'd heard so much about. It was like she was looking at movie stars. She asked if I thought she'd have a shot at one of their scholarships.

"Absolutely. Between that, fee waivers, and part-time work, I don't think money will be a big deal. Stuff like what happened this morning, that'll be more of a problem."

"I think you're right."

"The racism was always there for the people I talked to. Even the ones who had mostly positive experiences."

We walked and crossed Speedway Boulevard. I told Gabi about Richard Davis, who finished his bachelor's in 1969. He was offered a job at IBM before he graduated, but a supportive professor talked him out of taking it, saying he had the potential to do better. At the same time, some teachers told him the only thing he could become was a teacher, preacher, or athlete.

We passed the fountain outside Old Main. A dog yelped and bit at the falling water. A wind hissed through the palm trees as we passed through the main gate onto Park Avenue, a jumble of cars. Gabi asked how Richard Davis did.

"He graduated and went on to law school," I said. "But some classmates suggested he was only there because he was black. Same thing when he got his first job clerking. But he still graduated with honors."

"Some of these people, I don't know, they sound tougher than me."

We took a table at Geronimoz. It was semi-yup, lots of brass and glass. It had a long bar and tables spread out along the length of the narrow room. At happy hour it's crammed with students looking to get happy. But now it was early and mostly empty, a good time to talk. I had more transcripts in my bag, stories of the black experience. We read them over hot chili soup and mesquite-baked pizza.

THE CLASSROOM EXPERIENCE

Elgie Batteau, 1930s

We had one teacher who was teaching a class in education that we had to take. There were two other black girls in the class. When we went in, he seated everybody alphabetically, A and Bs to the front and the X, Y, and Zs to the back the first half of the semester. But he sat the three of us together. The first girl's name started with L, Laos. She was from Florence. The other girl was from Phoenix. Her last name was R, Rogers. And my name at that time was Mike, M-I-K-E, and mine was M. He sat the three of us together and left a vacant seat between the girl's name who started with L and the next person. We were the only three blacks in his class.

When the first half of the semester was over, he reseated and put the X, Y, and Zs to the front and the A, B, Cs to the back. But he left us where we were.

There were always two or three, maybe more, of the white students who would come to us and say, "Let's go to the dean and tell the dean about what's going on." They said, "We'll go to the back along with you."

We would say, "We have a hard enough time as it is. They have accepted us. And we are just trying to make it. So if we started going to the dean, it may stir up more trouble."

The only D I have on my record, he gave me. The three black girls that were in his class, he gave us all Ds. The dean of the College of Education told me, "Ask him to let you see your bluebook and go over your bluebook with him."

I asked the teacher, "Where was I weak?" We had four questions and four points to each question. I said, "Did I fail all of them that I should get a D?" He gave each one of us a D, and we had been getting Cs and occasionally, he would give us a B.

He said, "You were weak on one point of one question."

I said, "And that deserved a D?" The dean had kind of coached me on how to handle it. I said, "I would like to see my bluebook. Can I make an appointment with you to go over it together?"

He said yes. He made the appointment. But when I went up for it, he said the janitor had thrown his bluebooks away, and he didn't have them. That is the only D I have on my record. He gave each one of us a D. But we had to go through all of that.

I had one professor, and she gave me a B as a final grade. I said, "I am happy to get this B." I had been so accustomed to them giving me Cs, you see.

And she said, "Well, you deserve an A."

And I said, "Well, I would have loved to have seen an A on my grade sheet."

She said, "But I had been told not to give a black student an A." They said, "If they were very good, give them a B. Never give them an A."

I was so happy that they accepted me because they weren't accepting you every place then. Blacks weren't accepted. They didn't think we had the intelligence to do it.

Mildred McKee, 1930s

I was the only black person in most of my classes. It wasn't uncomfortable. The only place I felt really uncomfortable was in the classes where the teachers segregated. I think his name was Larson. He taught education. He segregated the blacks in the class. He sat everybody alphabetically. But the blacks in the class, he sat alphabetically together in a row. He would usually skip a row then would seat all the whites alphabetically.

But he was very democratic about it. One semester he would seat us all in the front and then the next semester in the back. I remember in one class, I was the only black, so he sat everybody alphabetically, then skipped a seat and sat me, and that ended the line.

Laura Banks, 1940s

I had some bad experiences in humanities where I made Ds every time. I think I had a prejudiced professor because a couple of times, I compared my paper with some of my white friends, and the answers were so close. We had our own style of writing, and they made good grades, and I made bad grades. That told me that he could just care less about me being there. I had to take humanities over twice. I believe I failed it that first time. The second time I made a D. I believe that is the only course that I ever made a failing mark in that I can recall.

Anna Jolivet, 1940s

I remember one experience that I had with a speech class. The professor said to us when we started that she wanted each of us to make a tape. "I'm going to analyze the tape and talk about the kinds of things you need to do to improve your speech."

She was going to give us something to read when we did this taping. We all went over and did our tapings and came back. A few sessions later when she was analyzing the tapes that had been done, she called my name, and I raised my hand. She said, "Oh, did you do this tape?"

I said, "Yes I did."

"Well, I'm surprised. I did not find anything to correct in your speech."

I just looked at her and thought, "Well, what did you expect? You were anticipating. From looking out over the class, you had identified who you were going to have major problems with, and here I am, and I have given you a tape, and you have not found anything incorrect in my speech."

In one of our education classes, the professor was saying that if the legislature passes a bill to do away with segregated schools, part of that would say that teachers would be assigned to teach in any schools.[5]

Here we are all in the same class, learning the same kinds of strategies for instruction, and the question was raised, "If our schools were desegregated, and if you had black teachers assigned to teach in any school, how many of you believe they would be effective teachers?" Only a few hands went up.

Then, "How many of you feel the instruction would be inferior?"

There were all these hands waving saying that this was their belief.

One of the people that was in that class with me, I know she doesn't remember me from that class, but years later we taught together in the same school, and then I became the principal where her son went to school. She was very complimentary of me as a teacher and also as a principal.

I thought, "You don't remember when we sat in class and you raised your hand and said you didn't think black teachers could be effective teachers."

I don't think that at the time I was enrolled there was an expectation that I would ever teach anywhere but in a school for black students.

I don't think I ever heard or saw anything that made me believe that the professors were looking at me or any other black student to say, "You will be an asset in improving relationships and contributing something significant in that area."

Cressworth Lander, 1940s

I didn't want to be a teacher. I'm a businessman. At the University of Arizona they said, "We don't have people like you in business school. Are you sure you don't want to be a teacher or a preacher?"

When Morgan Maxwell Jr. and I would sign up for a business class we would have to hear, "Gee, do you really want to take a business class? Don't you want to be a teacher? Marketing and banking? Do you really need to be taking these classes?"

I didn't do very well at the University of Arizona. Not very well.

Weldon Washington, 1950s

There was a course in Health Ed that got to me. This guy, he was always talking about these diseases. And he would always say something about the high incidence of specific diseases in blacks. That really got to me. I never said anything. I don't know why. He gave these lectures and always said something about the high ratio of blacks having these diseases. Any type of disease would be more prevalent in blacks. It was a tremendous course. I made a B in there, then an A.

Malachi Andrews, 1950s

I was an art major. I was probably the first black person ever to graduate from the art department. I was the only black in the whole art department when I was coming through here. I talked to the instructors more than I did with the students. I didn't really have any art friends.

Well, in anatomy, Dr. Quinn was talking about, here's the kind of nose that you do for colored people, and here's for Chinese, Asians, and here's for Europeans. And everybody's looking at me, cause I'm the only example. And then some student's looking over and says, "He screwed up there."

My hair was nappy. Stuff like that. It was kind of embarrassing to me. Because the language then was "colored," and all of that, and I'm the only one sitting there in the class that the students had to look at and that threw them off. My lips were big, my skin was dark, my hair was nappy, but my nose was not . . . see. He was going by the textbooks about different cultures, and most cultures felt real bad about that.

And he didn't need to do that in my mind now. If he was sensitive, I wouldn't have even taught that lesson like that and used the word. But in those days, it was all right then, 'cause I wasn't a human.

Ernie McCray, 1960s

The only thing I can remember was about attitude. And I could easily be accused of crying racism.

I was taking a political science course and learning about how a bill becomes law. I remember bringing up our struggle in class regarding what we were trying to do with the Tucson City Council and the prof said, "Well, that is of no concern here." To me, that would have been a time for some real learning to happen in the classroom. I still haven't had a real need to follow a bill through Congress.

We were about the only ones who were aware of racism at the time. You know, blacks and Latinos. And that's the way it was. We had discussions about being angry. Telling somebody how pissed off we were.

Even though you knew you couldn't go into restaurants, there was something in you that made you try it every now and then. You just feel like you need to be able to walk through that door. And you try it some place. And over and over again, "We can't serve you here."

Olden Lee, 1960s

I do remember some prejudice against athletes from professors, but it was in a different context. It's how they acted when they saw you in a particular class. In the 1960s most of the blacks on campus were athletes. If you had some size, they knew who you were.

I feel, because I was taking accounting and statistics, chemistry, psychology, it was a bit like, "Why are you in these classes?"

And when you would raise your hand to answer a question or to raise a question, the expression they would give. It was like, "Why are you . . . I am not sure I want to hear what you have to say." I distinctly can remember that.

Now, they didn't say that. It was just a perception I had. But it was never, "I would like to hear what you have to say. I appreciate your opinion on this." It was almost like if you sat there and said nothing, they would never call on you unless they were trying to show you up.

FINDING A PLACE TO LIVE

Elgie Batteau, 1930s

Tucson felt like the Deep South, like Texas, very prejudiced. I had gone in Litt's Drug Store by the Woolworth's and gone to the counter and they waited on me. But if I went in with my black friends that I had, they wouldn't wait on us. They ignored us. We would stand there or sit there. Sometimes we were just trying them out to see if they would do that. That was in the city. We had so many problems because they weren't serving us in the commons on the university campus.

Black girls couldn't stay in the dormitories. It was lucky for me that my aunt lived here, and we had the lower floor in the Steinfeld home. We had our two bedrooms and a little living room and everything. I didn't have to go through that embarrassment of trying to get in the dormitories.

I didn't know what dorm rooms looked like, but there was a girl here from New York. She was in one of my classes, and she lived in the dormitory. She invited me to come in, and we would study for tests and so on. I was a little reluctant to go in. She said, "Well, you are going in with me." The matron never said anything to me, but black girls could not stay in the dormitories.

Gabi shook her head. "That's just ridiculous. I can't believe that stuff happened."

Anna Jolivet, 1940s

The university held a full week of freshmen orientation. We took a variety of tests and heard numerous lectures for all of the freshmen about university life.

There were classes that all of the girls took, I don't know about the boys. Orientation extended throughout a semester. This was to teach you about living away from home and being more independent.

I found that much of it did not apply to black students. They had a rule that if you were a freshman female student and you came to the university from a city outside of Tucson, you must live on campus in one of the dorms.

We had black female students that had been coming from other places for years. They were not allowed to live in dorms on campus. They had to seek housing with families in the community.

Nobody seemed to think about how ridiculous their orientations were. Things that they were saying only applied to the white students that were in attendance. It was not for the rest of us.

Malachi Andrews, 1950s

When I got here, they took me over to East Stadium. There was a big room. I walked in this room, and there was two other black people. That was all. A big ole room. All these beds like the army. Cots up and down. All of a sudden, there was this football player, Don Beasley, and Hadie Redd and myself.

We was sitting in there. We all met each other. I had my Bible with me. Hadie Redd asked me, "You a preacher?"

Beasley was a big ole fullback. Hadie Redd was a tall basketball player. I was this little ole guy with a Bible in my hand. They called me Prof for Prophet. "Hey, Prof."

It was kind of weird, the three of us. Beasley was in early training. You saw all these other athletes at West Stadium. There was a west wing and an east wing. Everybody else was there, and you walk down this hall and there's all these athletes, all these white guys. And you go over to another place and you see all these white people. You don't see no black people around. Then when we go back to go to sleep, the three of us are there.

I'd never experienced that before. Something was happening. Why do you have three black people in the dorm, and no black people nowhere else?

That first semester there was three or four of us in that stadium. We stayed there for about three weeks. Then they moved me to Navajo Hall. I went in there, and I was rooming with a guy from Los Angeles, and we got on real well.

But the people next door. You hear, "There's a nigger living next door," or, "Yeah, we got darkies in Navajo Hall."

Now I'm hearing these sounds, and I say, "OK. I'm in a whole different land," and I started thinking race. I started thinking race for the first time in my life.

I tolerated it until I finally got up one day, after hearing these ethnic slurs, went out here and knocked at the door and said, "Look, you have a problem with me?"

He said, "Oh, no, what's the problem?"

I said, "Well I keep hearing you talking about 'niggers,' and using words that I don't think is nice."

He said, "Oh no, did you say that?" And they all started laughing. So now they're gonna laugh at me.

I go back to the room. I wanted to change my bed, but those

beds were locked in. So I just never stayed in the dormitory much. I just went to the library. I just went back there to sleep.

Lena Jones, 1990s

Until my year, in orientation, they only talked about the white Greek organizations on campus. White Greek rush. Socially, in a lot of ways, you're invisible.

SWIMMING

Laura Banks, 1940s

I majored in physical education. It was my second major when I was getting my elementary education teaching certificate. One of the required courses was swimming methods. They didn't want me to take it. I was told I could not take that. I said, "But I need it if I am going to get my physical ed certificate." I still couldn't take it. Every time I tried to register for it, I could not get it.

My mother got pretty fed up with that. She went with me to Ina Gittings, who was the director of the entire physical ed department, and she said, "Laura needs this. I have paid the money for her to get her certification and she has got to have it."

We threatened a suit. In fact, we had already alerted the NAACP that we thought we had a pretty good case and we wanted them to follow through on it with us.

Ina called in the P.E. teachers who taught swimming. They had this little meeting with closed doors in there. It ended up that one of the instructors went out to the pool and asked those girls out there if they minded if Laura swam with them because she needed the course. It was tragic.

EARNING AN HONEST DOLLAR

Anna Jolivet, 1940s

There were no black people employed at the university when I was in attendance. It was announced in one class that if any student needed employment, we should go to the university employment office for students and let them know that you needed employment. They would try to see that you were employed somewhere on campus so that your working hours could be worked around your classes. They assisted in that way.

So I went to apply. When I went in, the person in charge said, "Yes, may I help you?"

I said, "I came to apply for one of the jobs that are available to students."

"Oh. Well, we don't have any jobs for you."

I asked, "Well, don't you have jobs for students?"

"Well yes, but we can't give them to Negro students."

Malachi Andrews, 1950s

Hadie Redd and Don Beasley were on the football team. I'm on the gymnastics team and on the track team and an art major. I didn't have any grade problems. I'm going to class and everything.

Hadie and Beasley, they would take a art class, and I would help them straighten their lettering out or help them in their classes, tutoring.

What they would do for me is we would go down the food line, and I would give them my tray. I would buy some milk, or buy some bread with my tray, and then I'd take it to the table. They could eat all they want. It was like a smorgasbord for them, 'cause they was on full scholarship. So Hadie and Beasley would get a big ole plate and then go sit down. And then they'd dump the food. They'd share with me, and then they'd go back for seconds. I mean it was survival that year and we had to take care of each other. I was the only one not on scholarship.

They claimed that no track person had a scholarship, and I wasn't a protester, but there was about three white athletes that was on full scholarship, and I was the best athlete all of a sudden, and I'm starving to death. So that started to bother me.

My first argument was with Mr. Cooper, my coach. He came in the gym and says, "Well, I'm trying to get you a job," just kind of cold. He had a deep voice. I was very despondent, 'cause they told me I can't live in the dormitory 'cause I can't pay.

I was just going to classes normally 'cause that was no problem registering, and I says, "Well how can I pay that if I don't have a job?"

And he says, "Well I'm trying to get you a job, but you won't take the jobs I'm trying to get you."

And I says, "You want to give me a eat-a-meal, work-a-meal job." He wanted me to go down to the Pioneer Hotel.[6] I'd go down there for lunch. I'd work a hour, and I'd eat. I said, "That's not a job. How am I gonna pay my dormitory? How am I gonna pay all this here with a eat-a-meal, work-a-meal job? That's not a job, Coach."

He said, "Well, that's about all I got right now. You don't want it?"

And that's the first time I ever said to an authority, I said, "Ram it."

I remember those little words. He just walked out. I was despondent, and then he came back later and got me a dog racing job. Those were the best jobs among all the athletes. I got a job as a photo runner. All I did was take the photos back and forth. That was a big-time job.

Ernie McCray, 1960s

My high school girlfriend was pregnant, and so I was an eighteen-year-old parent when I started at the University of Arizona. By the time I graduated, and I graduated right on time, I had three kids.

We got married maybe a month or so after my oldest daughter was born. I was working odd jobs, and fortunately, my scholarship was a full one.

But there again, racism finds subtle ways to play. People of influence who could have given me some real good kinds of jobs asked me how I played basketball, raised a family, and studied, instead of helping me out.

They had these real cushy jobs that football players got. Watering trees for a ridiculous amount of money. And Enke[7] could have helped me get one of those jobs if he shined it on. When you are struggling for a little dignity, you would like to have a good job as compared to pushing a broom or something like that.

LOOKING BLACK: TEACHERS

Mildred McKee, 1930s

There were no African American teachers at the time. I don't remember one. I didn't think about that.

I can't think of any professors who went out of their way for me. One, I think, was Dr. Walker. He never bothered with doing segregation. There was a better feeling in his classes, as far as I was concerned.

Laura Banks, 1940s

I don't really remember one single person who reached out to me when I was just down in the dumps, and there were many days that I was. I didn't know how I was going to make it, and I needed extra money for gym fees or something, and I didn't have it. I wasn't sure how my mother and father were going to get it. I can't think of anybody. Isn't that sad?

There's no one that sticks out in my mind at the University of Arizona. And it's too bad. I just can't think of who my support system may have been in those days. I just cannot think of it. And I don't forget when people are nice to me.

Richard Davis, 1960s

I abhor the fact that when I was in school there were no African American professors whatsoever. And there still aren't any.[8] We have a few officials out there. I don't think that the university has done a whole heck of a lot to more or less recruit any.

GOOD SPORTS

Cressworth Lander, 1940s

Texas Tech[9] comes to town, and they won't play "with niggers on the team." And the coaches went along with that stuff. Fred Batiste didn't play in the game.

Malachi Andrews, 1950s

There was other guys that came in. You always got good people. You focus on the good people. Bill Smitheran, Larry Brown, they were in my dormitory. There were some good, good people in the dormitory. That overshadowed those people that was causing the problems.

Hadie Redd, 1950s

The thing is my teammates. Bill Reeves, Larry Brown, George Rountree. These guys were so interested in me making the team. I was concerned that they would often post-up to make sure that I would do well. Without them, I wouldn't have made it. They made sure that I did well. Not only that, they wanted me to excel.

We had a good start. We won three of four games at the beginning.

I remember as if it were yesterday, the late coach, Fred Enke, after practice, called me over. He said, "Hadie."

Oh God! I thought I had done something wrong. One thing he didn't want us to do was dunk the ball. He'd always tell us to use the backboard. I thought maybe he had seen us doing some clowning. He'd always insist that we use the backboard. He always said, "What do you think the backboard is for? Be sure you use that thing."

He called me over. I walked over to him, and he had his head down. I remember this. He placed his hand on my shoulder. Something was on his mind. I could read that automatically.

He says, "Hadie, we are off to a good start, and I don't know how to put this to you. Please believe me that I tried everything I could. We are going to Lubbock, Texas, and I've tried everything to find a hotel that will accommodate the whole team." He said, "The answer is all the same. 'No.' I want you to go, the team wants you to go, and basketball wants you to go. It would be good for the state too. I want you to think about it."

I commenced to walk away. I thought very quickly and I said to myself, I says, "I'm here now," not realizing that my entry onto the basketball team was making history. I wasn't thinking about that. That was the furthest thing from my mind. I didn't think about that at the time. As I began to walk away, I says, "My God, I can't let someone else do this. I'm here. I have to take on this challenge. I just have to do it."

As I was walking away, I called to the coach, Fred Enke. I says, "Coach." Then I walked back over to him. I says, "Let's go. I'm ready." It seemed as though there was a lot of weight lifted off his shoulders.

I called my dad, he was alive then, and I told him the decision I had made. He applauded me for that. He told me, "I know it is going to be a very difficult task for you because I know you have never been confronted with anything like this because as a kid, you were sheltered by your parents and protected."

And I says, "Do you think we should tell Mom about it?"

He says, "Son, it is up to you, but if I were you, I would not mention this to your mother."

I said, "Why, Dad?"

He said, "If you did, Arizona would be minus one basketball player and that would be you."

I never told my mother about it until after this was all over.

1954, Lubbock, Texas.[10] Texas Tech. We arrived at Lubbock, Texas. Got off the plane. Got on a bus to go to the hotel. Upon leaving the bus, all of the men were getting off and going into the hotel. I walked up the steps and proceeded to go into the hotel, and a doorman placed his hand on my chest. He says, "You can't come in."

I had to wait outside. I went and sat on a bench along with my coach and some of the other players who were ready to strike. They didn't want to play. They says, "We don't have to take this."

I encouraged them. I says, "We came down here to play the basketball game and try to win and do our very best and get out."

But I couldn't react. Everything would have been destroyed and that was not what I wanted to do, and I am sure that this isn't what the other fellows wanted to do. There was very serious talk about not playing the game as a result of having to be separated.

You go on these trips, and you get picked out by a black family. Beautiful people. They want to do everything they can to make you comfortable. Anything you want to eat you can have it.

I recall leaving the hotel. Once the car started to leave the hotel, I would always automatically look back at that hotel and wonder how the other guys were doing. And it really wanted to bring tears to your eyes. I tell you, the loneliest thing in my life.

But upon arriving there, in Lubbock, Texas, I stayed with a doctor, Dr. Miner. Very nice person. He has a hospital there. A small hospital. That's where I stayed. Upon arriving there, I can recall that he made me as comfortable as anyone could.

We visited some black elementary and high schools there, and I chatted with the students. But at nighttime, your mind is so entangled that you can't think right. It just blows your mind, and you try to lie down, and you can't lie down. You try to watch TV. It doesn't work. Radio doesn't work. You are saying to yourself, "What have I done? Out of all the teaching that my mother and father gave me, my teachers, my coaches, the whole lot. The olive branch. None of that's working. None of that's working."

But it just petrifies you to know that you have to be split off from your team and treated as though you were someone from another world. It's not easy. It's not easy. But I tell you, that hand on my chest, I still feel the imprint on it.

Ernie McCray, 1960s

I was recruited to play basketball by a couple places, but the University of Arizona didn't go after me. But Allan Stanton met me at the Y after my senior year, and we did some one on one. He was a graduate student then and the freshman basketball coach.

They didn't recruit black players much. I was the only one from my team. There were two other black players my sophomore year, and they quit at about mid-semester. Eddie Mitchell and Elmer Green.

Hadie probably had to stay at people's homes when he played teams in Texas. When I got there, that was no longer in existence. But you could still feel the tension in places.

I remember our first year going to Texas Western,[11] I believe. I was in a room, and I had a roommate, but it was a tacky room. I can't remember who was rooming with me, but I went into other rooms, and they weren't as tacky. It was like nobody had slept in there since George Washington, and it looked like they hadn't even changed the linen, even for George.

I didn't have a car, so after basketball practice at the University of Arizona I used to run or jog home. It was just quicker. I showered after practice, and I just wanted to get my thoughts together. I would say three times a week I was stopped by cops.

"What you running from?"

I remember once coming from the Stone Avenue underpass,[12] and some people drove by in a car and said, "Hey, you nigger" or something like that.

And I said, "Fuck you."

And a cop was there tending to a dog that was hurt in the street, and he said, "Hey, you can't talk like that on a city street."

I said, "Hey, they were yelling at me."

And he said, "If I wasn't tending to this dog, I would haul your black ass into jail."

Olden Lee, 1960s

I was committed to going to college and getting a degree. But I must have thought about transferring about fifteen times, and the athletes talked me out of it. There were a couple of times that I had a bad experience with one of the coaches and said, "That's it. I know he wants me to go. That's fine, I'm leaving."

And the guys would come into my room and say, "You can't do that. We need you on the team. Don't let this guy get to you."

But there is only so much you take. And I think towards the end, it became a personal challenge to beat it. But I thought about leaving.

Richard Davis, 1960s

I remember once being involved in a drill and hurting my ankle after another player, who happened to be Anglo, had done the same thing. The coach suggested that I was faking and forced me to drill anyway. And quite frankly, I told him where he could go. One of the things that made me a little different is that I didn't mind telling coaches that. I didn't need him and maybe that is one of the reasons why I may feel slightly different.

I gave up athletics after my first year. I did it largely because I thought that the way the African American athletes were being treated at that time was horrendous. Plus the fact that they passed the GI Bill the next year and I didn't need to play athletics anymore. Had it not been for that, I would have done whatever I had to do to go through school.

Gabi waved a breadstick in the air. "I seriously don't know how they lived through this. I would've been in my room crying all the time. At least they got revenge."

"How so?"

She shrugged. "By succeeding."

"I thought so, too. Then I read a passage from Bell's book, *And We Are Not Saved*. It hit home for me how deep and long-lasting the pain can be."

I recited the passage from memory: "I recalled the lectures over the years in which I had attempted to explain to mostly unbelieving white audiences how vulnerable to the smallest aggressions of racial fear and hostility even the most successful black person remains. Income, professional achievements, and prestige—none of these is a certain defense."[13]

The people I spoke with talked about how they dealt with the emotional component of racism.

FEELINGS

Mildred McKee, 1930s

Segregation hurt. It is a sort of conditioning you get. If education hadn't been a very important part of my life, I probably would have made more of a fuss about it. I look back on it, and I wonder how in the world I did it.

I didn't think it was right, but I think I saw it as something I had to get through. My parents would always say, "Get your education. No one can take that away from you." I remember that. They were always supportive of us.

I give my parents credit because they gave me a lot of love and a feeling of self worth. None of us liked the racism. We all objected to it. But no one got organized enough to do anything about it.

We talked about it. We talked about how unjust it was. We were all just wanting to get our degree and get out of there so we could go on about our business. I am sure some of them participated in some things. But not to the extent that a person would if they were really involved in the school.

Most of us were determined to get through. Some of them did drop out to take jobs. I think most of us had the determination to finish and get our degree and get on out of there.

Anna Jolivet, 1940s

Of course it hurt. I didn't go home and cry. I guess I feel worse about it now than I did then. Thinking about it now, I am angry that I did not express great rage then over the inadequacies.

Cressworth Lander, 1940s

There was no open door anywhere for blacks. You lived in the community, and you went to school just like you go to night school or something. You were not really part of the campus life.

We staked out the fountain and that became our headquarters. Other people had dorms and sorority houses and other places. No social life on campus at all. Except at the fountain. Everything was in the town. Everything was in the town. We had to stake out the fountain at Old Main. The fountain was our domain.

Ernie McCray, 1960s

I was cheered at Bear Down Gym, but the racism was always there beyond Bear Down.[14] Not being able to eat in restaurants around town.

I remember talking around that time to the guy who started the Big Boy's hamburgers nationally. Johnny's Big Boy or something. I cursed him out because he said, "Well, Ernie, I don't know about blacks being able to eat in restaurants, but you can." Special dispensation. Screw you.

I know what it was like for those blacks who attended the University of Arizona in the 1930s. It was the same as it was for me.

If you are catching it anywhere, then it all has a bad taste to it, if you can't eat at a restaurant. There were places in Arizona where you couldn't buy gas.

You are always aware of color.[15] People say that black people are so color-conscious. They are always bringing up racism. The reason is that our color is always brought up to us. We see a lot of racism. Sure, there are some false claims now and then, but not that often.

You're born, and you come out into the world, and people start calling you names. It is really hard on kids. You can't quite figure out what this is. I can't remember a time in my life where my color wasn't an issue.

Johnny Bowens, 1970s

Loneliness, feeling a sense that we didn't really belong here. You're still feeling that there is still some racism that was happening at the University of Arizona.

"Niggers." I heard that and, "Why are you here? Why don't you go back where you belong?" And when we came together to compare notes, we found that it was more common. It wasn't just an isolated instance in terms of faculty treatment. The policies that the university had, you couldn't relate to. There was nothing there culturally that we considered African American or to relate to our particular needs and wants.

Lena Jones, 1990s

My roommate was also black. We were at a football game. Some guy took out a black blow-up doll, and he was behind my friend and I, and there was a hostile exchange between my friend and this guy. You know how they bounce beach balls around the stadium? This doll was just flying around the stadium with people batting it around. That had a really deep effect on me. It's funny, I didn't realize how deep it affected me until a couple years later. Just seeing that image of a black woman being batted around by a bunch of white people was very, you know.

I guess one thing that made me get involved in a lot of different areas, too, now that I reflect upon it, was the fact that my friends ended up chasing the guy out of the stadium, and they chased him *out* of the stadium. But I was so paralyzed with shock that I didn't do anything. I've always wondered why I didn't say anything.

Later I wrote a letter to the editor responding to another letter to the editor in which a guy wrote saying, "Why are people making such a big thing about this incident? It was just a joke." I wrote explaining why it wasn't a joke and how it makes other people feel. My mom was afraid for me being out here by myself. I let her convince me not to send it in, and I've always regretted that.

It's a different kind of racism now, one that is harder to fight. It's not blatant. It's not people openly calling you this name or that name. It's a racism that's harder to prove that it's actually happening. But it's still just as hurtful. It hurts.

Gabi shook her head. "I believe that."

"Hidden, but still ugly," I said. "Let me show you something Derrick Bell said about this." I reached into my shoulder bag and found my copy of *Faces at the Bottom of the Well: The Permanence of Racism.* I flipped to page six and read aloud:

Racial bias in the pre-*Brown* era was stark, open, unalloyed with hypocrisy and blank-faced lies. We blacks, when rejected, knew who our enemies were. They were not us! Today, because bias is masked in unofficial practices and "neutral" standards, we must wrestle with the question of whether race or some individual failing has cost us the job, denied us the promotion or prompted our being rejected as tenants for an apartment.[16]

"So he's saying racism will always be there," says Gabi.

"Yes. In some form or another."

We paid the check and left Geronimoz. It was a nice night, a black sky, the moon, air that felt clean and good to breathe. Traffic had thinned from the late-afternoon rush. Now the worst we had to worry about was a pair of skateboarders doing their high-wire number on the sidewalk. We parted for two of them. They passed in a wooooosh. Gabi watched them disappear. Then she had a question.

"You said before that the college experience for Mexican Americans was different. Tell me about that?"

I explained how G. A. Larriva, a 1925 graduate of Nogales High School, talked about a clear-cut caste system at the university in those days. Anglos came first, then Mexicans, Latin Americans, maybe Jews, and way down on the list, Negroes.

Then there was Nazario Gonzales, who started college after Larriva graduated and said Mexican Americans were still treated with disdain. When Gonzales out-performed another student on an assignment, the student shot back, "At least I'm white." Gonzales didn't know what to say. He only wanted to fit in and thought of himself as white, too.

Others said the class differences that existed among Mexican Americans were obliterated once they reached the university, where they were all considered, simply, Mexicans.

Carlos Vélez-Ibáñéz, a 1961 graduate, described paying summer visits to relatives in Sonora. His family there was well-off. "I learned quickly that there was a class distinction," he said. "They didn't call it class. They called it money." In Tucson, the number of distinctions multiplied. A kid from the Mexican American south side could be poor but come from a good family. *Buenas familias.* He also described the *cremita,* the solid upper class. But during the academic year, the only classes that mattered were the rich and the poor, and the Mexicans and non-Mexicans.

Gabi and I sat on a bench outside the university's art museum. The day's sunlight was falling away, tossing its pretty shadows onto the tall statue hovering over us. It didn't occur to me until we sat down how fitting this spot was for our discussion. The statue is a woman—either Native American, Spanish or Latin American, it's hard to tell—cupping both hands to her cheeks in a gesture of fret. Given our discussion, I considered remarking on the symbolism of that. But I decided to leave that to the English majors.

I had a quote from Carlos Vélez-Ibáñez in my bag. I read it aloud to Gabi:

> I remember taking a Spanish class here. I was eighteen years old. I don't remember her name. She said to the class in English, "None of you *mexicanos* can expect to make better than a C because you all come from a mongrel group."
>
> There were three or four Mexicans in the class. A mongrel group? So we look at each other and we say, "*Qué es esto de mongrel?* I know mongrel means dog." And we say, "*Está loca?*" That she is nuts.
>
> I stuck around in the class for a little while and she repeats the same thing. We come from a mongrel group and we aren't going to get any better than a C. So I decided, Hey, I'm not going to stay in that damn class. So I left.

That was my first introduction to an actual verbal announcement of how little value we were at this university because we were Mexican.

They always wanted you to write about Hester Prynne or *The Pearl,* or they wanted you to write about the American notion of how the world worked. Never about your experience as a person or your parents or anything else. Well, a Mexican from the south side making 75 cents an hour isn't going to do that. I wrote about *La Llorona*[17] or fighting Irish kids on Congress because they thought we were Italians and called us wops, or hunting lizards, or hunting snakes out there at Midvale Farms, or going to Cat's Back Mountain at midnight to see if *El Vaquero* would come down. That they wouldn't hear.

It was customary for you to introduce yourself in class. As soon as you say Carlos Vélez-Ibáñez, voom, you get these stares. Oh. He's one of those. You could see it, feel it, and taste it.

"Why can't we all just be Americans?" Gabi asked.

"Good question. A lot of other Americans with brown or black skin would like to know the answer to that, too. It seems like citizenship alone doesn't meet the definition. But blonde hair, blue eyes, and money does."

Edward Ronstadt, class of 1938, preferred to be known simply as "American." His family was part of Tucson's upper class. Whenever someone asked if he was Mexican, he said he was an American of Mexican descent.

Gabi asked if he was related to Linda Ronstadt.

"He's her uncle."

"Cool."

Even for some of those who said they experienced no racism, their description of their lives suggests otherwise. For example, Richard Salvatierra, class of 1943, said, "In those days, the university was viewed as an educational system designed primarily for Anglos, and you sort of accepted it that way." Others made similar remarks. Patricia Williams wrote about it in her book:

It is not that we are all that rare in time—it is that over time our accomplishments have been perceived as 'firsts.' I wonder when I and the millions of other people of color who have done great and noble things or small and courageous things or creative and scientific things—when our achievements will become generalizations about our race and seen as contributions to the larger culture, rather than exceptions to the rule, isolated abnormalities.[18]

"But the situation for minorities got better over time, right?" Gabi asked. "I mean, it had to."

It did generally. But I explained that a slide-back seemed to occur in the 1950s, caused probably by a couple of things. The Brown v. Board of Education Supreme Court ruling was in 1954. The Korean War allowed record numbers of Hispanics and blacks to attend college on the GI Bill, raising their profiles on campus. And McCarthyism. All that brought racism to the forefront.

Marty Cortez-Terrazas was student-teaching at that time. Her supervisor told Marty that she didn't want a student helper but was forced to take one. The relationship deteriorated from there. The teacher made it clear, without actually stating it, that she didn't like Mexicans.

The following year a friend of Marty's, who didn't look Hispanic, was assigned to the same teacher. At one point, the teacher, assuming she was speaking to another Anglo, said, "I don't know why these Mexicans try to become teachers. They just don't have it." Deana quit on the spot.

Vélez-Ibáñez described the university in the late 1950s as a southern school that allowed Mexicans and blacks to attend. Derrick Bell made the same point when one of his characters said, "We are treated as aliens in our own country. Rather than view our ability to survive in the new land as a major victory for America, whites see it as a loss for them and a dangerous advantage for us."[19]

But students in the 1960s were more willing to speak up.

Activist Sal Baldenegro and his followers asked university President Richard Harvill how many Mexican American students were enrolled. He said that information wasn't available. They got a student directory and counted the surnames. They quit at the Martinezes after counting about 200. They asked the director of the Student Union to include Mexican songs on the jukebox at Louie's Lower Level. They also wanted Mexican music in the Union study area, a place where a student could borrow headphones and listen to songs.

"Who's going to listen to Mexican music, for God's sake?" the director said.

Frank Felix remembers feeling alone in a sea of Anglos. When he took sociology with a hundred other students, he felt intimidated as the only Hispanic. He sat at the back of the class and did poorly. After his first semester he wanted to perform better, so he moved to the front and was confronted with racial remarks. One student said he didn't know they allowed "spics" at the university. Felix stood his ground in the Student Union, too, when some guys tried to move him out of his seat, saying he shouldn't be there.

Frank worked in the financial aid office his junior year. One day the associate director called him in and said, "We want you to tell your relatives they're not going to get special treatment at this university." His boss was saying that Frank gave special treatment to Hispanics. Frank explained that Hispanics felt more comfortable coming to him. "We don't want you to spend so much time with Mexicans," the boss said. Frank quit his job on the spot.

Vélez-Ibáñez left the university but eventually returned to complete his degree. "I left without even withdrawing," he said. "I was pissed off at the chickenshit. I just got tired of it."

Gabi perked up at that. "Isn't there a difference between being a victim of racism and getting your feelings hurt by dummies?"

"Not if you're on the receiving end. What about what happened to you today?"

"Oh. Yeah. I see what you mean."

"But I'm still not sure if the problem is racism or discrimination by class."

We talked about Richard Gonzales, who did well in college and decided to go on to law school at the time the Bakke case was working its way through the courts.[20] Gabi had never heard of Allan Bakke, so I explained. He applied to and was rejected for admission to medical school at the University of California. He sued on the basis of reverse discrimination, saying he was denied a space in the class because the school accepted less qualified minorities. The suit, and the ruling supporting Bakke, intensified the affirmative action debate in admissions at colleges across the country.

The University of Arizona Law School was looking for Hispanics, and Gonzales was one of them. As a first-year law student, some of his white classmates refused to study or socialize with him. They believed he'd taken a spot that should have gone to someone with higher grades or better standardized test scores.

In 1972 during Gonzales's first year, a student sued the school alleging reverse discrimination, naming Gonzales and other Hispanic students as representative defendants. The student said he had the same or comparable GPA and LSAT scores, yet the minorities won admission.[21]

"So, Gabi," I said. "Gonzales got accepted to law school, studied hard, got through, and now he's successful. But did he suffer racism?"

She pondered. "You're right. It's complicated. When people make things tougher on you because of your race, yeah, I'd say that's racism. But it worked out okay. I don't know, it's confusing."

"It's even more confusing when you talk about Hispanics. Remember Rafael Gallego? Got laid off from the mines and got work as a janitor at Hughes before trying college? He really nailed all the complications we're talking about."

I pulled out the Gallego transcript and read.

Rafael Gallego, 1980s

All of a sudden I went from being the first in my family to complete a four-year degree to the first to go to graduate school. I started law school in September 1987. I remember, even though I had a degree, being careful about how I spoke, making sure that I had a decent command of the English language. You're with the cream of the crop there. In undergraduate school I was just one in 30,000. In law school you're one in 300. It's a small community. It's very intense. You're definitely a minority. You can feel it, you can definitely feel it.

Gabi spoke. "That's class, socioeconomic class, much more than race."

"Okay. What about this?"

I continued with Gallego:

Right off the bat, you're differentiated in the grading. I remember there was only one Hispanic that I know of who got real good grades his first year. The guy just had the Hispanic name. He had no idea about what that culture meant. He had no idea. I remember the other Hispanics talking about that. We were very happy for him, but he was not in tune to our culture. The rest of us fought tooth and nail for Cs.

There was tension between the traditional Hispanics and the non-traditional Hispanics. There were the Hispanics who even had a hard time saying their own last name. They were truly out of touch. We just couldn't stand those kind of people. We looked at them as sellouts.[22]

It was real unfortunate because here was an opportunity for a person, because of the way they progressed in law school, to become a role model for Hispanics yet to come. But they didn't want anything to do with it. So we were very angry. We should have looked at ourselves as role models,[23] but we didn't because we didn't do as well academically.

"How about that one?" I asked.

"Tricky," Gabi said. "High-class and lower-class Mexican Americans being mad at each other. I don't know if that's class prejudice or maybe reverse racism."

"There's more from Gallego. Listen."

> I used to hear all the time, "The only reason you're in is because you're Hispanic. You took the spot of a higher-qualified white." All the time. I don't recall any blatant discrimination from the faculty members. Just the students.

Gabi had a quick answer for that one. "Racism. Totally."

"Sure, but even that's complicated. I bet Anglicized Mexican Americans didn't hear those remarks. And I'll bet there was resentment by whites and even higher-class Hispanics when they saw a lower class of people joining the club."

I had more:

> I didn't feel I belonged there once I got in. I almost quit after my first year. It was just devastating.[24] You know, you go through undergrad, and you do real well in a short amount of time. All of a sudden you're in there, and you're working your butt off for a C. I think I got one C in my entire college career as an under-graduate. All of a sudden I'm getting straight Cs. It was awful.
>
> I didn't go to professors for help because that was way too scary. You already feel like you're at a disadvantage and going to them is almost like confirming that. They use the Socratic method, which meant the professors called on students. Unless I was called on, I never volunteered anything. I just felt that what I had to say was going to be dumb. Many times I would be thinking something, and another student would say it, and I'd think, "Well, that wasn't so dumb after all." But that first year was just incredibly humbling. I truly think that the way the questions are formatted or whatever, Hispanics have a harder time.
>
> Some of our classmates were second- or third-generation lawyers. A lot of these people have heard words like "trust accounts" before. I had never heard the word "trust" in that context. I'd heard the word "will." But some students had wills. They had trust accounts. They knew about stocks. They knew about bonds. Those were just words to us. They had an easier time putting them into context than we did because we never had to put them into context.

"Well," Gabi said, "that's class. Money. His family didn't know about money. But it's hard to blame it only on class difference. They could've been put in a lower economic class because of racism."

"Oh?" I wanted to draw her out, keeping her thinking on those lines.

"I'm trying to remember something I read. One of the critical race theorists wrote it." She paused. "Let's see, 'racism results in class stratification that tends to reproduce itself.'"

"You get an A plus. Anything else, doctor?"

She laughed. "As a matter of fact . . . What does class reproduction mean?[25]

"Once you're in a socioeconomic class, that's where you stay."

"But people move up all the time. Kids from my high school are doctors now."

"Think of it in terms of tendencies rather than rules," I said. "Sure, there's movement between classes. The critical race theorists wouldn't argue that. Most of them have moved up.[26] But what they say is it's tough and rare. Uphill all the way. Even in the job market."

I read Gallego's comments on his job-hunting experience:

> It's all a vicious circle over there. When it comes time to interview, you are not going to get one unless you are in the top third of your class. Because of differences in language or differences in upbringing or both, and other things in our culture, we don't do as well on tests. Because you don't do as well on tests, you are not recruited by the big, high-paying law firms. And if you get lucky enough to know somebody who knows somebody to get you an interview, the question of grades is going to come up and they're not even going to consider you.
>
> So you're left with trying to secure any job, even if it pays only one-eighth of what you could get in the law firms. All you are left with is the public sector, government work. The public defender's office, the county attorney's office, legal aid. Those are the only things that are left to us. After all, we do want to work.
>
> I had a discussion with a professor about my wanting to get a job at the DeConcini-McDonald law firm. He knew somebody there. He said, "What are your grades?" I told him. He said, "You know what? You'll never get a job there. Don't even try it. If a person gives you an interview, it's probably because he's nice. He doesn't know how to say

no. You'll never end up working anywhere except the public defender's office."

I was so insulted. I got out of there. I just left. He thought he was giving me good advice. I remember the next day I saw him, and he said, "I hope you thought about the advice I gave you." I dug into my pocket and gave him a penny and said, "This is what I think about your advice." I was really upset. I was livid.

I went to the county attorney's office instead. Even that has its own stigma. As a Hispanic you're expected to be a public defender. I remember other students telling me, when I was clerking at the D.A.'s office, "You've got to be kidding me? You should be at the public defender's office."

The shadows had lengthened, then darkened until the statue above us was invisible in the early night. But we felt its presence. Gabi remarked again how tough it must be and how much courage it must take for a minority student to endure and succeed.

"I don't want to feel hopeless, Jay." She stopped and tugged at a blade of grass at her feet. "But sometimes I do."

I had one more passage I wanted her to hear. It was from Derrick Bell. I thought it would make a nice close to our discussions, something she could mull over on the bus ride back to Nogales. I tilted the paper up and used the moonlight to brighten the type:

> The obligation to try and improve the lot of blacks and other victims of injustice (including whites) does not end because final victory over racism is unlikely, even impossible. The essence of a life fulfilled—a succession of actions undertaken in righteous causes—is a victory in itself.[27]

5 <

Activism   Gabi's desperation had changed by the time I
talked to her next. Now she was mad. The
stories of the African American experience at
the university had moved her, and she wanted
to know why they tolerated such treatment?
Why did they endure being treated as
"outsiders"?[1]

I told her she was right to believe that
many of my black informants had been passive
in the face of discrimination. But surely not all
of them. Some viewed activism and resistance
as important parts of their university experience,[2] even before the turbulent 1960s and
1970s. It was Derrick Bell—or specifically,
Geneva Crenshaw, his courageous and articulate protagonist—who ignited Gabi's passion.

"Geneva traveled the South risking her
life to change the system," said Gabi.

We were talking by phone. She was in Nogales. But her voice was clear and strong.

"But the people you interviewed, they took their places in the back of the classroom, turned in their homework on time, and prayed for the best."

"No, it wasn't like that at all, Gabi." I waited to see if my firmness bothered her. I don't think it did. She'd come a long way. "Several of them were active, outside and inside the system."

"Really? How?"

"I've been putting together some of their stories. How about I mail them to you. Will you read them?"

"Are you kidding? I love hearing about that kind of stuff."

THE COKE

Elgie Batteau graduated in 1935 and began work on her master's degree. One day while registering for summer school, she and a friend went for a Coke in the basement of the new women's building. But they couldn't get served. They waited more than twenty minutes. Finally Elgie stopped the waiter.

"We've been sitting here, and we'd like a Coke."

"Well, I have to wait on these other people," the waiter said.

"But we were here before they were, and we're thirsty, too."

The waiter promised to come back.

"I think you could get us a Coke for ten cents," Elgie said.

"A Coke for you would be seventy-five cents."

Elgie called the waiter's bluff. "We'll pay you seventy-five cents. We just want a Coke."

"It'll be five dollars."

"We'll pay you five dollars."

Elgie remembered some white students sitting nearby. They joined Elgie in confronting the waiter, threatening to report the incident to the summer school dean. The waiter got flustered. "You know, this isn't my lunch counter. I just work here."

The white students went to the dean, and he sent for Elgie. "The counter will be closed for three weeks," the dean said. "When it's opened, regardless of whatever you are, white, black, Indian, or Mexican, or whatever, you will have no more problems. It will never be closed to anyone else."

Elgie explained why she didn't push the issue herself. "We were having these problems the whites didn't know about," she said. "And we were just trying to get our work done and get out of the university and get work."

THE PLAYERS AND THE JOBS

Cressworth Lander came to the university just after World War II, and says he had little or no involvement in university activities. Even so, he remembers helping to elect Stewart Udall[3] as class president. Udall went to the administration to demand that black athletes be recruited and given scholarships. In 1948, Fred Batiste became the university's first black football player on scholarship. A few years later, Hadie Redd became the first black awarded a basketball scholarship.

Off campus, Cressworth was part of the Young People's Progressive Political Club. The group launched a voter registration drive among Tucson's blacks and pushed for jobs in county government. During meetings with the sheriff's department and the county assessor's office, the group demanded jobs in those offices. "We don't want any money," the group argued. "We don't want a bottle of wine. We want these jobs."

Says Cressworth, "We placed eleven people in county government in 1948 behind our Young People's Progressive Political Party."

THE SENATOR

Arnold Elias's activism flowered as a result of a class project. He and several friends had a special relationship with Political Science Professor Bernie Hennessey. The group had taken every course in the department, and wanted more. Professor Hennessey had an idea: "Why don't one of you run for public office, and when you're through, you can write a paper about your experiences. What happened? What did you do? What were the successes? What were the failures?"

Arnold became the group's candidate for senate. The incumbent was James Corbett,[4] an entrenched politico. Soon the students had a grassroots movement going in Tucson's Hispanic community.

"A group of about twenty or thirty of us got together and ran a campaign for the state legislature," Arnold recalls, laughing at the memory. "A whole lot of people came to our aid. Just Señor y Señora López who wanted to help. And before we knew it, we had a small army of people we could depend on. We won by forty votes."

Arnold Elias spent his senior year as a member of the Arizona State Legislature.

THE ATHLETE ACTIVIST

In addition to being a basketball star during his sophomore year in 1958, Ernie McCray was part of a small group called Students for Equality. He and Jackie Collins, a classmate, were the only African American members. Ernie remembers setting up a booth near the walkway at the Student Union.

"I got more hate stares than encouragement," he says. "I remember going down to talk to the city council and being gaveled down by Limey Gibbings.[5] There's a sucker I have no respect for. He wouldn't even let us talk. Called us rabble rousers or something. It was about racial issues. It was about opening up restaurants in town."

When Ernie left Tucson with a master's degree in 1962, some restaurants still didn't serve blacks. But it was okay for blacks to purchase take-out orders.

THE ORGANIZER

Salomón Baldenegro was raised to be an activist. He remembers his mother's advice: "Don't you ever, ever pick on anybody, and if I ever hear you do, I'm going to beat the crap out of you. And second, not only do you not pick on anyone, if you ever see anyone being picked on, you go and you intervene and you help that kid being picked on."

Sal's mother grew up in an orphanage and was considered unadoptable because of her dark skin. Not only was she a victim of severe discrimination there and in Arizona's foster care system, but her husband's family initially rejected her because she spoke little or no Spanish. "On one hand, she got it for being a Mexican," says Sal, "and on the other for being a gringa.[6] She got it from both ends."

It wasn't enough for her children to simply tolerate differences. They were expected to join any fight on the side of the victim.

Sal didn't complete high school on his first try. He returned as an eighteen-year-old and became friends with a buddy's dad. Maclovio Barraza was a Chicano union activist and founder of what is now the National Council of La Raza.[7] He was a miner and a regional director for the mine and smelter workers.

Maclovio was involved in union politics and was a member of the Viva Kennedy club, then the Viva Johnson club. He spoke to Sal about politics and shared books about political issues. But for Maclovio, politics was more than reading books and stimulating discussions. He dragged Sal to the Pickwick Inn, a Tucson restaurant that refused to serve blacks.

"Now, you're probably wondering, young man, why we're here," Maclovio said to his young protege. "See all these folks?

They're black. Now what are we doing here? We're Mexicans. Because if you let these people do this to one group, they'll do it to all of us. We're next. You see that sign? If they say, 'No coloreds,' the next sign you'll see up there will say 'No Mexicans.' That's why we're here. Now, get a sign."

When George Wallace and Lester Maddox spoke at the university, Maclovio and Sal were among the picketers. They also picketed outside Safeway grocery stores in support of Cesar Chavez's grape boycott.

Sal enrolled in the university, but after a year went to Los Angeles to join his mother, who'd relocated, and to be close to his girlfriend in Riverside. Sal remembers it as an exciting time:

"The high school walkouts were starting to develop.[8] There were Chicano centers opening up, Chicano newspapers. The Watts riots in 1965, 1966.[9] We drove my brother to work through Watts. It looked like a war zone. I mean, tanks were everywhere. The National Guard was out there patrolling the streets."

He attended a community college and was admitted to UCLA but didn't attend. He returned to Tucson after a year. "I came back home," he says. "And that's when I really became political."

Sal found that his immediate peer group at the university was less than enthusiastic about politics. They worried that if they started organizing, they'd be singled out, and that would make it harder to be accepted. "We will stick out," they told Sal. "Now, we can be hidden."

Sal was concerned about how few Mexican American students attended the university, and among those who did, only a handful came from Tucson's predominantly Hispanic public high schools—Tucson, Pueblo, and Sunnyside. He was also concerned about the working conditions of the campus gardeners and wanted to promote the grape boycott. But Sal failed to interest his friends in these causes and tried a different approach.

"We were all Catholic in our group," remembers Sal. "There was a very radical, very leftist national group called Young Christian Students. For a long time people thought that it was Young Catholic Students, but it wasn't. It was made up of Catholic kids, but it was called the Young Christian Students, YCS."

Sal went to the Newman Center and talked to the priest about forming a chapter of YCS:

"I went to the priest and said, 'Look, I am a university student, and I attend mass here.' It was a lie. I didn't go to mass there. 'And I'd like to form a YCS group. We try to get the gospels and apply them to our daily lives.' And he said, 'That's great.' So I told the kids about it, the Salpointers,[10] who were all devout Catholics. 'Hey, why don't we form a YCS group so we can do some real good things in the community.'

"I have to admit, I had a hidden agenda. My sense was to use YCS as a tool to politicize them.

"Well, we would go to the gospels. And we'd read them and discuss them. What does this mean? How does it apply to us? How can we put it into practice? I would always skew the discussion to a political interpretation. 'Well, yeah, you can say that the prodigal son means that you should respect your mother and father, but can we also say that the prodigal son could also mean that we should strengthen the family? One way we strengthen the family is by supporting the grape boycott.'

"They would say, 'How the hell did you get that?'

"I'd say, 'Look, guys, kids are having to drop out of school to pick those damn grapes, and mothers and fathers and pregnant women are out there being sprayed with pesticides. Now, don't you think kids should be in school, and mothers should be home baking cookies and so on?' I would somehow force an interpretation.

"Then how I finally got a lot of people to come over was to say, 'Look, guys, let's personalize this thing, the grape boycott. We are talking about farm workers here, and you people think the farm workers are in California and elsewhere. But they are not. They are here. Why don't we do a literacy project in Pascua?'

"They said, 'Wow. Teaching people English helps them.'"

The group's relationship with the Newman Center didn't work out. Sal and about a dozen of his friends left and formed MASA, the Mexican American Student Association. Sal's group was willing to follow him as long as it wasn't political.

MASA began much like several on-campus Hispanic organizations during the previous half century. It offered a supportive system, a social outlet, a sense of belonging and tutoring. Members spoke to Hispanic students at local high schools, encouraging them to go to college.

The group raised about $5,000, created bylaws, and gained university recognition. Initially, they were supported by older members of the Mexican American establishment, such as John Huerta, who endorsed the group's goal of increasing the numbers of Mexican American college students through raising money for scholarships and mentoring.

Even though MASA membership had risen to nearly sixty, many members felt Sal's views weren't representative. "I never stopped drifting to the left, and pretty soon MASA impeached me for being too radical because I was making speeches," says Sal. "I would get up at Speaker's Corner and speak against the war and for the boycott, and I'd speak against racism. By that time, I was talking about discrimination in the high schools and the lack of faculty. That had become an issue."

Sal resigned rather than be impeached. About a dozen people left with him and formed the Mexican American Liberation Committee, which evolved into MEChA,[11] a leftist, political group. MASA lasted for another two years. Sal and his followers found their strongest opposition from the next older generation of Mexican Americans. They wanted to take over the system from inside. But Sal said the system was corrupt, and once inside, it would corrupt you, too.

"You need to attack that animal from the outside," he argued.

Sal soon found himself on the receiving end of angry phone calls from Hispanic city leaders. Newspapers and TV began covering him, his group, and demonstrations they organized.

Other groups on campus were active as well, and they shared roughly the same beliefs—the Black Student Union (BSU), American Indian Movement (AIM), and mostly white antiwar students loosely affiliated with Students for a Democratic Society (SDS).

The Mexican American activists were against the war in Vietnam and pro-civil rights for African Americans, but were more focused on their own experiences with racism. Many recalled high school counselors steering them away from courses such as algebra and into studies more "appropriate" to Hispanics.[12]

Sal and members of MEChA met similar students from around the country, especially from Texas and California. "We didn't know each other. We had never talked to each other before, and when we were comparing notes, it was almost like we read the same book."

To bring those issues to public attention and try to change the way minorities were treated in Tucson's high schools, Sal and his group organized walkouts at Pueblo and Tucson High Schools. At the university, Sal and others questioned the admissions process and minority student recruitment. Admissions officers told them it did no good to recruit at Cholla[13] or Tucson High or Pueblo because those kids won't come here anyway. And if they did, they dropped out.

The Chicano activists found support on campus and around the country. After 1969, a coordinated national Chicano student movement pushed to establish Chicano studies. Chicano priests became active, too, including a group from Tucson—Fathers Alberto Carrillo, Ricardo Alford, John Shaughnessy, and Vicente Soriano.

On campus, Professors Adalberto Guerrero from Spanish, John Schwarz and John Crow out of political science, Roger Yoshino from sociology, and Cornelius Steelink from chemistry publicly supported their activities.

The students submitted a list of demands to the administration that included active minority student recruitment, a Mexican American cultural center, a dean of Mexican American student affairs, and a summer bridge program.

The administration approved New Start, a program to help students from disadvantaged backgrounds make the transition to the university. But the administration provided no funding, prompting several faculty members to come to the rescue. An engineering professor lambasted Harvill[14] in the papers, calling the lack of money an insult. "If you are going to create a program," he said, "you have to fund it." He found about ten other professors who gave $1,000 each to start the program.

After two years, Sal and members of his core group began to wonder what good they were doing in class, listening to Durkheim's theory of sociology and suicide, when they could be spending their energy organizing in the community. They had to make a choice.

"The grape boycott, the high school walkouts, organizing unions, all those things took us off campus," says Sal. "Academically, it hurt us tremendously. Politically, it did us good. To the extent that we represented the university, we made the university visible to our community. For one of the very first times, people in the barrios were seeing university students come out and do something. Be very visible. And not only being around at fiestas and at church and at stores, not only just physical. We were out there doing things."

Sal and several of his activist friends decided in 1971 to leave the university, without graduating, to become organizers in the Chicano movement. Sal completed his bachelor's degree in 1986, a master's in 1988, and now is pursuing a Ph.D. Others in his original group also finished college as adults.

WORKING THE SYSTEM

In 1966, Richard Davis helped form a University of Arizona chapter of Alpha Phi Alpha, the black fraternal group whose alumni include Martin Luther King Jr. and Thurgood Marshall. He was also president of the first Black Student Union and spent some of his Saturdays with families in Marana[15] talking about the possibility of college for children of farm workers. "We got some kids enrolled. Those kids graduated," he recalls.

THE BULLETIN BOARD

In the early 1970s, a group of Hispanic students, including Julieta Gonzalez, Tom Amparano, Frank Felix, Macario Saldate, and a handful of others, began to meet informally at a table at the Student Union. They came together initially for company. Completing their degrees was the top priority. Groups such as MEChA[16] didn't fit their taste.

"By then Sal Baldenegro's antics had become well known and well publicized," says Julieta. "The pictures in the paper showed him face down in the gutter with his hands in handcuffs. We said, 'That's not us. We don't have arrest records. We don't intend to become police blotter material.'"

"I couldn't relate to MEChA," recalls Evelia Martinez.[17] "Physically they chose to dress poorly. One of the things my mother had always instilled in me was pride in how you looked. You're always ironed. Your clothes might not be brand new or the top of the line, but they're always clean. They're always ironed. The *Mechistas* always looked terrible. They had the raggedy clothes and the unironed shirts, and they looked like they hadn't taken a bath in a week or two. I wasn't going to become part of that group. That was too much for me."

But the group eventually engaged in its own brand of activism.

It was spurred by the appearance on campus of a Mexican American speaker from the Civil Rights Commission that nobody came to hear. Word of the talk simply hadn't gotten around. Frank and Macario suggested a remedy to the communication problem: a Hispanic bulletin board in the Student Union. The students coalesced around the issue.

"We went through the Student Union, ending up at a dean's office to see if we could reserve a bulletin board," remembers Tom Amparano. "And they said no." That was enough to spur the group, now two tables strong, to form Concerned Chicano Students (CCS).[18]

Tom Amparano, a Vietnam vet who helped organize the first Chicano Business Students Association, remembers a feeling others had felt decades before. "We are almost invisible around here." He and others wanted to tell the university, "You have to start doing some things for Hispanic kids."[19]

As a means of raising its visibility, the group decided to run a candidate for student body president. Felix was close friends with a group of Anglo antiwar students who thought it'd be useful to have a sympathetic student body president. Bill White, a friend of Frank Felix's, suggested the group put forward a Hispanic candidate, preferably a female. "Somebody nonthreatening but intelligent," he said, "so you can really form the agenda she's going to impose."

The group picked Julieta, and she agreed to run. "These were older guys," she says, "and they said, 'She's young, doesn't know shit, gets good grades. She's very credible from an outsider's point of view. She's cute as a button, has great legs, and looks great in a mini skirt. She's enthusiastic. She's got lots of other friends we can mobilize.'"

Julieta realized that her level of sophistication regarding Hispanic issues didn't match theirs, but she was awakening. With Amparano as her running mate, they lost decisively. But Frank Felix said the election energized a lot of Hispanics, and the original two tables grew to five, bringing a sense of unity to some 200–300 Hispanics—all because of a bulletin board.

That bracing experience led to action on other issues, such as the recruitment of Hispanic faculty and students. Their first objective was an opening in the political science department.

"Macario Saldate and I walked into Cliff Lytle's[20] office and made an appointment for the next day," says Frank Felix. "Then we walked in with twenty people." They told Professor Lytle they were aware of the vacancy and wanted him to hire a Hispanic professor. Lytle said he intended to hire the best-qualified individual he could find.

The group threatened to remain in his office until he agreed to hire a Hispanic professor and allow them to interview the candidates. Lytle and his colleagues talked about university procedures, but the students refused to back down. Several candidates showed up for interviews, including one Hispanic. Frank remembers what transpired next:

"They weren't going to let us interview him. So we said we were going back into the office and sit there. We're not going to allow any function in the department to operate until you allow us to interview him. So on a Sunday, they said, 'Where do you want to meet him?' I said, 'At the Royal Inn, they have a bar there. We'll meet him there.'"

Three university officials joined about eight students at a table. The students were drinking beer. Everyone sat down and the head of the university delegation said, "Well, let's begin."

Frank answered for the Mexican American students telling the search team, "You're not welcome here. You'll have to leave." They acquiesced and left a nervous faculty candidate to be interviewed and evaluated by the students.

"We came back out and decided that he was not the strength that we wanted to have," Frank recalls. "We wanted someone who was really going to support what we were doing. But I said, 'Well, they brought him, they are going to offer him a job, so let's get on the bandwagon and support him.'" So we did. "The next day, Monday, we said 'Hire him.' They did."

Julieta describes the group's relationship with the university administration as antagonistic. "I remember specifically asking John Schaefer[21] and John Lesher, his attorney sitting at his right hand, for statistics on employees on campus," says Julieta. "Could they break it down for us? Were they professors, professional staff, gardeners? Schaefer turned to Lesher and said, 'Do I have to give them that information?' John Lesher just sat there and shook his head no. We never got it."

The group remained active and expanded its focus, advocating hiring a dean of students for Hispanic affairs, then Hispanic faculty in the Sociology and History Departments and in the College of Education. Tom Amparano chuckles about a photo and headline in the *Arizona Daily Wildcat* in which he remembers reading, "Chicano Students Storm Sociology Dept."

Frank graduated in 1972, and his political interests spread beyond campus. When he began studying for his master's degree, he decided to make a run at the Arizona state senate. A friend, an intern at the senate, invited him for a visit. The legislature was arguing a farm labor bill. Frank's reaction was swift and strong.

"Jesus Christ, they're stupid," he thought. "These guys are really not intelligent at all, and if they can get elected, surely I can."

He took on Limey Gibbings,[22] a long-term senator who was not only a longtime university institution but also a powerful member of the senate appropriations committee. After conducting a methodical grassroots campaign led by his classmates, Frank, at twenty-four, became the youngest individual ever elected an Arizona state senator.[23]

THE B.Y.U. PROTEST

Johnny Bowens came to the university as a graduate student in 1968. He credits roommate John Heard with turning him political. They formed a Black Student Union.

"I and the others felt a sense of isolation," says Bowens. "Also, when we looked around, when we went to all our classes, we see we don't have any African American instructors. So we sensed that we needed to address those particular issues and issues about the larger community, the issue of being treated as equal."

The group wanted to address the university's lack of sensitivity and lack of services for African American students. The university's initial reaction was positive. The group created a charter and bylaws and won recognition. But once they started questioning university policies regarding African American faculty and student recruitment, and making specific demands, things changed. As their campus support weakened, the group turned to Tucson's African American community for help.

"What we found out was that people like Ruben Salter,[24] A. Sparks,[25] and so forth, who attended the University of Arizona, was dealing with the same problems that we was addressing," says Johnny. "They had the same experiences about the loneliness, feelings of isolation, feeling that the university didn't want to deal with any of the problems they had as African American students."

John Heard emerged as the spokesperson. Johnny Bowens, who describes himself as shy and inhibited, became the strategist and theoretician. The group was vocal. "People considered it militant," says Johnny, "because we was calling President Harvill[26] racist and the administration racist because of their lack of support for African American students, their policies of not recruiting more African American teachers."

Several of the activist groups coalesced around the issue of whether the university should participate in intercollegiate athletics with Brigham Young University. Students objected to the Mormon practice, later repudiated, of forbidding blacks from becoming part of the Latter Day Saints priesthood. A large demonstration was held at Bear Down Gym[27] during a basketball game. Several students, mostly blacks, were arrested. Johnny Bowens was there:

"Initially, it was very peaceful. We was marching round and around, and we was trying to convince people not to go. And while people was going in, there was a sense that they are not listening, that we need to take a more direct response and we need to go inside. In fact, let's stop the game.

"That kind of heightened feeling got to the point that we found ourselves at the door of Bear Down Gym. And Swede Johnson[28] was there, and the campus police was there.

"It was a give and take about what you're doing. Supporting racism? Words got exchanged. Pushing happened. And everything broke loose. We went inside. John Heard.[29] Gale Dean.[30] Felix Goodwin's daughter.[31] Goodwin pulled his daughter off the floor.

"We walked in under the north basket. When we came in, the teams went back to their respective seats. And we also asked the basketball players to join us and not play. Half the team was black. They said no. They couldn't do it because they was afeared of losing their scholarships. But they said they would wear a black armband or black ribbon to show that support and some of them did. A couple of them did.

"We went on the floor, and we stopped. When we looked around, we were getting all boos from the stands, but no one came, so a couple basketball players asked us, 'You know, we have an opportunity to win this game, but we would really like if you'd sort of leave.' So we did."

Members of the Black Student Union felt the university was exploiting black football players, and they still sensed discrimination in the Greek system. Felix Goodwin, an assistant to Harvill and a retired Army officer, served as an intermediary to black students. He'd recently completed a doctorate at the university and believed in working within the system. He remembers spending a lot of time with black students, trying to moderate their actions.

"We had a lot of so-called activists. The people raising all this hell who couldn't understand that when it came time to negotiate, that they didn't belong at the table. For example, you have a bunch of white Ph.D.s and white leaders sitting on one side of the table, and you have some partially educated blacks or Mexicans on the other side of the table.

"I've seen it happen here in Tucson when the whites just said, 'Well, we'll give them this little bit,' and that was that. It wasn't until we were half way through negotiations that people realized that you need a man or a woman who is equivalent to the whites at the table in age, in education, experience, and so forth."

Goodwin also lectured them about power. "You can be in the street with the bottle, but this white man doesn't give a damn about you," he told the young activists. "Believe me, white Americans as a group have no reason to fear blacks. They have the weapons and the whole power structure including the law behind them."[32]

He was both an administrator who sympathized with the activists and an "internal" activist who sympathized with administration. A lot of his time was spent trying to keep black activist students out of jail and in school.

When Goodwin got word that black students had decided to lock President Harvill up in his office, he let student leaders know that state police would be waiting, and the students would be arrested. He suggested that white students should take the lead and the risk. The groups met. When morning came, the whites were across the street waiting for the blacks to "do their thing." The blacks later thanked Goodwin for the warning and admitted he was right. The whites were not willing to take the lead or share the risk. Goodwin watched black students present a list of demands to the president and watched the president ignore them.

Johnny Bowens says the militant blacks criticized Goodwin

privately but not in public. "We wanted some kind of unity, and he was the only African American administrator," says Johnny.

A QUESTION OF CATEGORIES

Evelia Martínez remembers her first protest. She was a freshman.

"A group of us decided we didn't want to be called Spanish-speaking or Spanish surname," she says. "When we filled in our little ID card we put ourselves down as 'other.' Whether or not that ever made any impact or not, we don't know, but for us, that was kind of a way of protesting, making a statement. We refused to be pegged for convenience.

"We had our own identity and we wanted to be recognized. I think finally the university caught on because they ultimately changed the cards so that Mexican American was one of the categories. Or Chicano. They had Mexican American, Chicano."

But Hispanics and African Americans weren't unanimous in their militancy. "I was as turned off by being told that I had to do something because I was Hispanic as I was by those people who told me I couldn't do something because I was Hispanic," says Richard Gonzales.

Jim Garcia, a 1975 graduate, didn't join any organizations on campus and recalls saying to an older, more militant Mexican American: "I've always pursued my life as an individual. I don't feel like I need a Chicano group or a MEChA or a LULAC[33] or any of these groups to help my cause along."

REFORMING THE SYSTEM

Lena Jones, a 1994 graduate, was active in the African American Student Alliance. "After some incidents and things started happening, I kind of wanted people to vent with, and to know that other people were going through the same things."[34]

That year she also joined a peer advisory program. Through that activity she learned of the Minority Action Council, a student government service whose purpose was to encourage minority students to participate in student government, volunteer at the culture centers, help with student retention, and represent minority issues within the student government.

"I guess by participating in student government I started meeting nice people who weren't black, and that kind of helped me get back my perspective again," says Lena. "In that way it helped a lot. I still kept my black friends though."

I next heard from Gabi by letter. She'd read what I sent her, and it changed her mind about the group I interviewed. I suspected it would. But more than that, she found their stories inspiring. They weren't willing victims after all.

Teacher planning day was approaching, and Gabi and her family were considering coming to Tucson. "I've been thinking more and more about finally applying to the University of Arizona," she wrote. "Could I stop by your office to talk over my application?"

"Absolutely," I said out loud to myself.

6 <

Outlook for the Future

Gabi sat at the conference table in my office. It was a scatter of papers, her university application, financial aid forms, and more. We sat quietly for a long time. I had my feet up and my hands folded behind my head, the picture of nonchalance. My head told me that Gabi was going to take her first real step toward college today by putting her name on the application. But my gut wasn't so sure. I kept feeling that maybe this was the day she'd decide it was all too much and back out.

Gabi thumbed through the university catalogue. "You know something, Jay? You're a pessimist."

"What'd I do? I was looking out the window."

"No, your views. You're too negative."

"I am?"

"Yeah. Listen to this." She read from the

catalogue: "The university strives to create a campus environment that understands, fosters, and embraces the value of diversity among students, faculty, and staff." She stared over at me, silently challenging.

"Don't hold your breath, Gabi."

"See what I mean?"

"Words are easy. Real life isn't."

"I think you're living too much in the past. These people you talked to, they've got you thinking it's still 1950. Things have got to be better now."

The people in my study spoke about that. But their optimism wasn't great. Richard Salvatierra said the situation changed after the Civil Rights Act[1], but it was a forced change. It didn't arise out of a sense of morality or good will on the part of Anglos. He sees far more racism today, on and off campus, than even six or seven years ago. Anna Jolivet said that blatant discriminatory practices still exist, and racist comments are still heard, just like fifty years ago.

Laura Banks put it poetically: "We have a long way to go before we get home. Things are better, but the university is not much better."

Gabi's brown eyes roamed the catalogue. "Okay, what about here? There's an office of African American Student Affairs, one for Native Americans and one for Hispanics.[2] They even use the word 'Chicano.'[3] You can't tell me you believe the university hasn't changed."[4]

Some, like Weldon Washington, might agree with her. He sees positive developments, thanks to affirmative action and the introduction of summer bridge programs.[5] Olden Lee points to the university's Mexican American president as proof of change in the right direction.[6]

Hadie Redd, the pioneer black athlete in the 1950s, now a police detective in San Francisco, says that simply watching black and white players on basketball courts across America is a step forward. I remembered his quote: "Just maybe, maybe we started a flame here. Just maybe, somebody may have heard our voices. Just maybe we may have started something that needed to have been done a long time ago. Maybe we didn't set the world on fire, but somebody heard our signals. Somebody saw or heard."

Gabi liked that. "See. It looks to me like people saw and heard just fine. All the things minority students wanted in the 1970s have happened." She dragged a finger over the tip of her tongue and peeled back another page in the catalogue. "This talks about an African American Cultural Resource Center and a Chicano/Hispanic Student Resource Center. And I was reading in here that the percentage of minority students has never been higher."

When it came to arguing her point, Gabi had a stubborn streak. It was frustrating at times, but I also knew it would stand her in good stead if—when—she got to college.

"Programs are fine, Gabi. Pretty rhetoric is fine. But people are telling me it's not enough."

Johnny Bowens, the professor at Pima Community College, says minorities at the university are still cut off from the mainstream and view the cultural centers as a refuge[7] in a hostile environment. They still feel isolated. They still experience unequal treatment from professors. Some feel the only reason minorities are there is because of the color of their skin. "I'm getting a sense that people are concerned about physical violence against them," says Bowens. "That's the same feeling I had in 1968, 1969, 1970, and here we are in 1993."

Gabi dropped the catalogue on the table with a thud. "If he's right, what do we do? Just throw up our hands and let the strong survive?[8] That's the problem I have with the critical race theorists.[9] They're good at pointing out problems, but they don't have solutions."

"You're not the first to say that.[10] But don't be too hard on them. They've made a big contribution just in providing a new way to analyze the problem."

"You mean listening to minorities."

"Exactly. Like it says in the introduction to *Words that Wound*.

We have to use the experiential knowledge of people of color in analyzing society.[11] That's what you and I have been doing. Trying to find answers. Trying to find ways to make a better future."

"Don't get me wrong, Jay, I've enjoyed it. But I don't think we've found any answers. It's so frustrating."

This was a moment I feared. I knew how hard it had been for her, listening to so many problems and so much hurt. It was that way for me when I first did my research. But it's something we have to plow through. We have to see past it. That can be daunting to a teenager—to focus on the goal, not the hurdles.

"You liked the people I interviewed, right? I don't mean just that you liked listening to them. But you like them as people."

"Sure. I feel like I know them. Laura Banks, Cressworth Lander. Heck, yeah."

"And you trust them?"

She rocked her head, pursed her lips. "Yeah. I hadn't thought of it that way. But, yeah."

"How about trusting them to help with the future, too?"

"What're you talking about?"

"I asked every one of them what we should do next, what steps we should take. What they said, it was pretty basic stuff."

Gabi was eager to hear. She put down the application form and leaned forward. Her concentration was complete.

"First, they said racism was simply a permanent part of American life. We need to recognize that, continue doing what we can to fight it, and move on—the same view espoused by the critical race theorists. My black informants were especially insistent on the prevalence of racism.

"Next, they said that parents and family matter most, and that kids need early exposure not only to the possibility of college but to the necessity of it. As lawyer Richard Gonzales says, 'If there's any way we can ensure or enhance our kids' potential for success, it's going to come from within the home and having parents take an active role in their children's lives.' "

"Well . . . " She swallowed back whatever it was she was going to say. This was no time to hold back. I wanted to hear it.

"My parents, they're great and all. But they never went to college so it's hard for them to help me in this. I feel bad for them because I know they want to. They're as scared as me. I was thinking about that yesterday."

I told her the influence can come from outside the family, too. Alfredo Márquez remembers going to play golf one day with two other fellows. They needed a fourth, and were joined by a Hispanic man in his middle or late thirties. He introduced himself to Márquez and said he used to caddie for the judge in the early 1950s. "You were my role model," the man told Márquez. "I used to go home and tell my mother that I wanted to go to college and be like you[12] and be able to play with these Anglos and be on the golf course." That man is now principal at a local school.

Mike Duran said the key was exposure. He still remembers a law student who came to visit his class in high school. Duran liked him and began hanging around with him. The two even went to court together. "I just think the more experiences we can give young children, the better off they will be," said Duran. "Higher socioeconomic kids get that from day one."

Richard Salvatierra and Arnold Elias pointed to APEX as a significant aid in helping minority students eventually try college. The program introduces the idea of college to younger students and continues with advice and encouragement through high school. "I think exposing students to role models, nurturing, and getting to people at the junior high school level are the benefits," says Arnold.

Others believe the outreach should begin as early as fifth grade. Richard Salvatierra says college administrators give themselves way too much credit for getting kids through school. He believes the most significant influences come much earlier. Rafael Gallego says people from the community should talk to grade school children.[13] Speaking to them in Spanish is critical.

"Every chance I get, I'll go out to an elementary school, talk to fifth graders, because I think that's the key grade," he says. "Just speak to them. I purposely speak proper English and articulate something. And then I'll get into my Spanish. Then, one on one, if necessary, I'll even talk slang with them. It's so important. I don't want them to think, 'The reason he's where he is is that he's not in touch with us.' Once they feel that type of interaction and hear me talk slang with them, it throws them back. It's incredible."

Alfredo Márquez spoke about role models. "Sitting around the nineteenth hole, I was saying, 'Have you seen the Nike ad with Barkley saying, I'm not your role model?' I felt that ad was wrong. Let's face it. You're a role model whether you like it or not. Kids are going to look up to you if you are a famous person, if you are a top notch basketball player. If you are out there advocating the use of drugs, you are conveying a wrong message, whether you say you are a role model or not. You are a role model. You've got to use role models to set an example for people. That's one thing the universities could do. I don't know the specifics, but you've got to go out and teach kids that it is important to get an education. That there is some sacrifice. You are going to have to work. And what the alternatives are."

Finally, my informants unanimously agreed that a lack of cash, rather than racism, was the primary deterrent to higher education for minorities. "It all boils down to money," says Mary Jo Yrún.[14]

Willie Cocio says the question is more complex than the ability to pay tuition any given semester. It's about socioeconomic class. "I mean, you see your dad building houses and hey, that's your dad, man," says Cocio. "He's the coolest guy in the world. I want to build houses, too. There's nothing wrong with being a mailman. You don't have to be a doctor. But the kid whose father is a doctor says, 'I want to be a doctor just like my dad.' It's the same thing."[15]

Johnny Bowens has thought about these issues his entire life. He believes society is run by class. "If I go up to Skyline Country Club, I'm not going to be welcome there," he says. "But I also know that if a poor white goes there, they're not going to be welcome either. Race is used as a tool to keep people fighting amongst each other. I have more things in common with a middle class or poor white person than I have with the upper class. I am also aware that a middle class or poor white has more in common with me than the upper class too. That's the way I think race is used."[16]

Laura Banks believes it's about class, too. "If you come from a family that has a lot of education or has a lot of money, you probably have traveled a great deal," she says. "Travel really broadens your horizons. I've always said about white families, those kids learn more at the dinner table than some of our kids learn in five or six years."[17]

Gabi grinned. "I've never been anywhere. And I have no money. I guess that makes me a two-fer."

I laughed. But it was a serious point: without money, every other question was moot. She stared at the application form. "They want my e-mail address. Oh, seriously. That's really going to make kids from the barrio feel like they really belong."

"Good point. In fact, several of the people I interviewed talked about just that, but from the opposite point of view. While they might have grown up poor, their own children today enjoy a lot of advantages coming from families with education and money, including computers and e-mail addresses."[18]

Richard Gonzales, who remembers being intimidated by the thought of asking a law professor a simple question, says his children won't endure the same embarrassment. "We've had the chief justice of the Arizona Supreme Court at our house several times," he says.

"Superior Court judges come and have dinner and drinks quite often. We've had congressmen and senators in our house. They've known my kids since they were young. When my kids go to school, that'll make a world of difference."

Gabi fingered the application, and for a moment I thought she was going to grab a pen and finally begin filling it in. But she paused and glanced at a copy of Derrick Bell's book, *And We Are Not Saved.* She stared at it for a good long time. I was doing my nonchalant act again. But inside I was thinking, "Pick up the pen, Gabi. Pick up the damn pen." But she needed more time to talk.

"I still don't know if I'm brave enough or tough enough to do what those people did, Jay."

I told her she was. But I don't think she heard me. She pressed her lips together.

"But I really want to continue my education. I'm good at school. I've been working and going to school for two years already, and my grades are good. The race thing, I don't know, I think I can deal with that. I hope I can just be me."

On her own, she got up and went to my stack of transcripts. She fingered through them until she found what she wanted. It was another page of words from Richard Gonzales. Without any prefacing remarks, she began reading:

"I never had any notion that I could fail at something. It was just something from the way my mom and dad raised us. If you want it, and you will work at it, it is there.

"The one thing my dad drilled into my head, all of our heads, was that if you can work harder than the person next to you, regardless of where you are at, you will always have a job. End of story. Bottom line. You work harder. And that's it. It's that simple. And if you have a dream, don't let anybody take it away from you. Just go for it and work hard at it."

Gabi looked at me. "You know who that makes me think of? My great-grandfather, the Buffalo Soldier. I visited his grave again before coming up here this time."

"Yesterday?"

"Yeah. How'd you know?"

"Earlier you said you were thinking about your parents yesterday, how hard it was for them that they couldn't help you with this decision."

"That got me thinking about my great-grandfather. Being a black soldier back in those days. I read up on the Buffalo Soldiers."

"Oh?" Grab the pen, Gabi.

"The Army gave them rotten food, broken-down equipment, old horses, the toughest assignments. And they still served. They still won decorations for bravery and stuff. They did better than the rest of them."

"Yup."

"My great-grandpa, he was a tough guy."

"I'll bet." The pen, Gabi.

"The way he lived, the things he went through, it was a lot tougher than going to any college."

"Uh-huh."

"I've been thinking maybe it's in my blood. That I've got some of him in me."

"Do you think so?" The pen, the pen.

"I can work, Jay. And college is my dream."

She flattened her palm on the application form and slid it closer. She stared at it for a full minute before taking up the pen and beginning to write. It was like I wasn't even in the room.

Line seven on the application said, "Ethnic background: Federal law requires the university to report the ethnicity of all U.S. citizens and resident aliens in the following five categories: Hispanic; African American; American Indian or Alaskan native; Asian or Pacific Islander; White."

Gabi paused there, bit the end of the pen, and circled the word Hispanic. Her eyes jumped up to meet mine, and a glimmer appeared in them. Then she circled African American, American Indian or Alaskan native, Asian or Pacific Islander, and finally White.

She looked at me again and broke up. We both laughed from our hearts, me and Gabriela Valenzuela of Nogales.

< Informants

Name	Birthday	Entered College	H or AA	Parents Ed.	Value Ed.	Degrees Earned From Univ. of Arizona
Genero A. Larriva	8-30-08	1925	H	<HS	Y	BS Business Administration 1929 / JD Law 1967
Elgie Mike Batteau	b: 1-24-05 d: 4-13-94	1925	AA	<HS	Y	BA History 1935 / MA History 1945
Nazario A. Gonzales, Jr.	9-17-12	1934	H	<HS	Y	DNG / Agronomy
Mary G. Ott	5-12-14	1931	H	<HS	Y	BAE Spanish 1935
Edward F. Ronstadt	4-12-16	1933	H	<HS	Y	BA Political Science 1938
Mildred Hudson McKee	b. 10-3-18 d: 5-25-96	1936	AA	COL	Y	BAE Elementary Education 1940
Richard C. Salvatierra	7-29-20	1939	H	COL	Y	BA Journalism 1943 / MA Journalism 1977
Laura Nobles Banks	6-29-21	1939	AA	<HS	Y	BSE Physical Education 1943 / MED Elementary Education 1966 / EDS Educational Administration 1970 / EDD Educational Administration 1981
Mary Jo Lemas Yrún	12-18-28	1946	H	COL	Y	BSH Home Economics Education 1976
Robert M. Figueroa	12-18-19	1939	H	HS	N	BA Economics 1948
Alfredo G. Márquez	6-30-22	1946	H	<HS	Y	BA Economics 1948 / JD Law 1951

Name						Degrees
Mario A. Yrún	7-26-25	1946	H	COL	Y	BSB Personnel Management 1949
Arnulfo D. Trejo	8-15-22	1942	H	<HS	Y	BAE Spanish 1949
Anna M. Jolivet	11-24-28	1946	AA	<HS	Y	BAE Educational Administration 1950; MED Elementary Education 1965; EdS Educational Administration 1972; EdD Educational Administration 1976
Cressworth Lander	5-15-25	1946	AA	HS	Y	DNG
Weldon A. Washington	1-27-24	1941	AA	COL	Y	BAE Elementary Education 1951; MED Educational Administration 1955
Hadie Redd	4-13-33	1951	AA	—	—	DNG
John L. Huerta	2-24-32	1950	H	<HS	Y	BA Spanish 1955
Malachi Andrews	b: 9-11-33 d: 8-94	1953	AA	<HS	Y	BAE Art Education 1956; MED Secondary Education 1962
Martha Huerta Elias	6-19-34	1952	H	<HS	Y	DNG
Elena Preciado Navarrette	7-29-37	1955	H	HS	Y	BA Creative Writing 1974; MLS Library Science 1976
Marty Herman Cortez	3-22-36	1954	H	COL	Y	BAE Elementary Education 1958; MED Elementary Education 1970; MED Counseling/Guidance 1976

H = Hispanic descent; AA = African American; <HS = neither parent finished high school; HS = at least one parent finished high school; COL = at least one parent attended or graduated from college; Y = sensed a high value of education while growing up; N = did not sense a high value of education while growing up; DNG = did not graduate.

Name	Birthday	Entered College	H or AA	Parents Ed.	Value Ed.	Degrees Earned From Univ. of Arizona
Richard E. Pesqueira	5-7-37	1955	H	COL	Y	BSE Physical Education 1959 MED Educational Administration 1961
Arnold R. Elías	7-7-33	1951	H	<HS	Y	BA Political Science 1959
Ernest C. McCray	4-18-38	1956	AA	COL	Y	BSE Physical Education 1960 MED Elementary Education 1962
Diego A. Navarrette, Jr.	9-12-37	1957	H	<HS	Y	BA English 1960 MED Higher Education 1962
Carlos Vélez-Ibáñez	10-27-36	1954	H	HS	Y	BA Government 1961 MA English 1968
Salomón R. Baldenegro	1-14-44	1965	H	<HS	Y	BA Spanish 1986 MED Special Education 1988
Felix L. Goodwin	11-24-19	1964	AA	COL	Y	MPA Public Administration 1965 EDS Educational Administration 1974 EDD Educational Administration 1979
Olden C. Lee	10-16-46	1964	AA	HS	Y	BSB Personnel Management 1968
Richard Davis	9-12-43	1965	AA	<HS	Y	BSP Government 1969 JD Law 1972
Frank J. Felix	1-29-47	1968	H	<HS	N	BA Government 1971 MA Political Science 1967 PhD Educational Administration 1979

Name	Date	Year	Ethnicity	Parent Ed.	Value	Degree(s)
William J. Cocio	1-5-42	1960	H	<HS	Y	BFA Studio Art 1971
Johnny W. Bowens	6-2-46	1968	AA	<HS	Y	MED Educational Administration 1973
Thomas M. Amparano	9-10-47	1966	H	<HS	Y	BSP Public Administration 1973 MPA Public Administration 1980
Richard J. Gonzales	3-5-50	1968	H	<HS	Y	BA Government 1972 JD Law 1975
Julieta S. Gonzalez	1-11-52	1970	H	<HS	Y	BA Political Science 1973
James A. Garcia	6-9-53	1971	H	<HS	Y	BSB Personnel Management 1975
Evelia Martínez	2-21-52	1970	H	<HS	Y	DNG—Business Administration
Michael J. Duran	11-12-55	1981	H	HS	Y	BSB Regional Development 1983 JD Law 1986
Robin Lemon	1-15-62	1981	AA	HS	Y	BA Political Science 1990
David R. Carranza	9-7-57	1980	H	HS	Y	BSB Personnel Management 1983
Rafael F. Gallego	3-24-59	1984	H	<HS	Y	BSB General Business 1986 JD Law 1990
Lisa Watson	1-31-65	1983	AA	COL	Y	BA Journalism 1988
Lena Jones	10-26-71	1990	AA	HS	Y	BA Interdisciplinary Studies 1994

H = Hispanic descent; AA = African American; <HS = neither parent finished high school; HS = at least one parent is a high school graduate; COL = at least one parent attended or graduated from college; Y = sensed a high value of education while growing up; N = did not sense a high value of education while growing up; DNG = did not graduate.

PREFACE

1. See Loevy, *To End All Segregation.*

2. Slaughter, "The 'Official' Ideology of Higher Education."

3. Delgado, "The Imperial Scholar Revisited" and "Storytelling for Oppositionists and Others."

4. Aleinikoff, "A Case for Race Consciousness."

5. Crenshaw, "Foreword: Toward a Race-conscious Pedagogy in Legal Education"; and Culp, "Autobiography and Legal Scholarship and Teaching."

CHAPTER 1

1. The Iowa Tests of Basic Skills and the Iowa Tests of Educational Development achievement test batteries were routinely administered to Nogales, Arizona, public school students, many of whose first language was Spanish. For a discussion in support of the predictive validity of these tests, see Ansley, "Relationship of Elementary and Secondary School Achievement Test Scores to College Performance."

2. It is not unusual for American Hispanic people of Mexican descent to refer to themselves and other Mexican Americans as *mexicanos.* Conversely, they often refer to all Anglos as *americanos.*

CHAPTER 2

1. While there exists a varied literature on college student persistence and attrition or departure, I found very little literature that especially addressed minorities or that in particular attempted to describe when or how the possibility of a college education arises for them. The following are relevant to the question: Henson, "The Minority Pipeline"; MacDermott et al., "The Influence of Parental Education Level"; J. S. Davis, "Parents: The Hidden Resource" and "Athletics as Academic Motivation."

2. Pima Community College, a large two-year college in Tucson, offers classes and a small number of degree programs in Nogales, Arizona, as well as in other southern Arizona communities.

3. Camp Stephen D. Little was active between 1910 and 1931. It was named for Stephen Littles, a private who "died 26 November 1915, from a gun shot wound in head received in action against Mexican soldiers at Nogales on

26 November 1915." The post was named in his honor in 1915. Littles, a member of the 12th Infantry, was likely white because black soldiers served, at the time, only in the 24th and 25th infantries. The name of the camp was misspelled, and it was never corrected. Source: Unpublished memo by Orville A. Cochran, post historian, Fort Huachuca, Arizona, April 24, 1961, University of Arizona, Special Collections Library. For a lively accounting about an incident at Camp Little, see Wharfield, "Border Fight at Nogales."

4. For discussions about achievement based on individual merit and effort on the part of minority individuals see, for example: Carter, *Reflections of an Affirmative Action Baby;* Steele, *The Content of Our Character;* Rodriguez, *Hunger for Memory.* A provocative counter statement to much of the rhetoric presented by the above authors was given by Patricia Williams during the U.S. Senate Judiciary Committee hearings on the nomination of Clarence Thomas to the Supreme Court when she said (Sept. 17, 1991): "While self-help and strong personal values are marvelous virtues, they are no stand-in for zealous protection of civil and human rights. The problem with Thomas's espousal of self-help values is that he positions them in direct either/or tension with any other value. Self-help is presented as bitterly competitive rather than in complete concert with those social remedies and measures that would help ever more rather than ever fewer people." (Quoted from Hammonds, "Clarence Thomas and the Academy.")

5. With only two exceptions, all of my African American and Mexican American informants volunteered that education was a primary value that they remembered their parents trying to communicate.

6. Five out of 16 (31 percent) of the African Americans in my sample said at least one parent had been to college or graduated. Among the Mexican Americans in my sample, five of 29 (17 percent) made a similar claim. More notable, among the Mexican Americans who commented, 19 (66 percent) claimed that neither parent completed high school.

7. Seventeen (59 percent) of my Mexican American informants claimed an early awareness of the possibility of college. Twelve (80 percent) of the African Americans in my sample claimed an early awareness of the possibility of college.

8. The parents of the individuals I interviewed placed a very high value on education. However, the parents often were frustrated by their own lack of knowledge of the educational system and how they could help their children. This finding was similar to that reported in 1992 by Commins in "Parents and Public Schools." Shoemaker (1986), in a paper presented at the Annual Meeting of the National Association of College Admission Counselors, discussed the problem specifically with respect to the admissions process. She suggested that both parents and students should be taught the "technical vocabulary" of the process beginning as early as elementary school.

9. Bell's most recent book is *Confronting Authority: Reflections of an Ardent Protester.*

10. Delgado is the Charles Inglis Professor of Law, University of Colorado; J.D., University of California at Berkeley, 1974. Delgado created Rodrigo Crenshaw, a fictional character upon whom numerous discussions about race and law are based. For example, see Delgado, "Rodrigo's Fifth Chronicle."

11. Crenshaw, "Foreword: Toward a Race-Conscious Pedagogy in Legal Education."

12. Williams, *The Alchemy of Race and Rights: Diary of a Law Professor.*

13. See note 4. Also for a discussion of the "necessity" of affirmative action in higher education see Sowell, "Affirmative Action Reconsidered."

14. Hacker, *Two Nations.*

15. See note 4. One of the most interesting aspects of the information I gathered was the convergence, in my informants' perceptions, of attitudes supported by both the left and the right political points of view. On the one hand, they tended to agree that racism and discrimination were endemic to American life; on the other hand, they believed—and claimed themselves as evidence—that in the U.S., education through persistence, focus, and delayed gratification can afford an individual a better life. For an excellent discussion of this theme and other points of convergence between current left and right commentators, see Delgado, "Enormous Anomaly? Left-Right Parallels." For a discussion from the liberal perspective, see Freeman, "Racism, Rights and the Quest."

16. Carter, *Reflections of an Affirmative Action Baby.*

17. Steele, *The Content of Our Character,* p. 173.

18. Entered the University of Arizona in August 1932.

19. See note 7.

20. See note 1.

21. See note 1.

22. Low expectations on the part of both classroom teachers and counselors was a recurring theme in the interviews I conducted. For a discussion of this ongoing problem, see Hawkins, "Pre-College Counselors Challenged"; Parker, "An Awareness Experience"; and Smith, "Developing Career Cognizance."

23. See Dilanian, "The Influence of Peer Group Pressure."

24. See note 8.

25. Nineteen of my twenty-nine Mexican American informants (66 percent) said that neither parent had completed high school.

26. There is a large "A" built of boulders on Sentinel Peak on Tucson's west side. Each September the seniors would march the freshmen to "A" Mountain, as the students called it, to whitewash the "A" as an initiation rite.

27. Tucson's afternoon newspaper.

28. *The Arizona Daily Star,* Tucson's morning newspaper.

29. There is a rich literature dealing with the first-generation college student. However, little addresses the specific problems of minorities, and much of the literature focuses on the transition from high school to community

colleges. For example see Richardson, "Helping First-Generation Minority Students"; London, "Transformations: Cultural Challenges Faced by First-Generation Students"; and Prett, "First Generation College Students."

30. The students in Sunnyside High School, located on Tucson's far south side, are predominantly Mexican American.

31. Richard Gonzales was probably referring to the Kuder Preference Inventory.

32. See note 8.

33. See note 22.

34. See note 8.

35. Salpointe Catholic High School, Tucson.

36. See note 1.

37. See note 22.

38. At the time, the Cleveland Indians baseball team conducted spring training in Tucson.

39. See note 1.

40. Alfredo Márquez grew up in Globe, Arizona, a small mining community about 100 miles from Tucson.

41. See note 8.

42. The word "barrio" roughly translates as "neighborhood." In Tucson's early years, different neighborhoods became affectionately known by their "barrio" nicknames.

43. See note 8.

44. See note 22.

45. Pima Community College, Tucson.

CHAPTER 3

1. For an interesting discussion of this and related topics, see Attinasi, "Getting in: Mexican Americans' Perceptions"; and Christie and Dinham, "Institutional and External Influences."

2. Bell, *Confronting Authority*, p. 78 and p. 176, note 16, addresses this question and suggests that, for example, many of today's affirmative action hiring policies, while nominally ensuring racial, ethnic, and gender diversity, simply serve to maintain the status quo with respect to social class: "Historically, for instance, law schools campaigned vigorously against the establishment of night schools, which would open the profession to those unable to attend law school because they had to work for a living." Another factor present in his discussion was gender, which was not within the scope of this study.

3. Steele, *The Content of Our Character: A New Vision of Race in America*, expresses the dilemma from a middle-class black perspective: "Class and race are both similar in some ways and also naturally opposed. They are two forms

of collective identity with boundaries that intersect. But whether they clash or peacefully coexist has much to do with how they are defined. Being both black and middle class becomes a double bind when class and race are defined in sharply antagonistic terms, so that one must be repressed to appease the other" (p. 96).

4. Francisco "Pancho" Villa (1877–1923) was a Mexican revolutionary and bandit, a hero to some and criminal to others, depending on which side of the Mexican revolution people found themselves.

5. Porfirio Díaz (1830–1915) was president of Mexico from 1877 to 1880 and 1884 to 1911.

6. Face a firing squad.

7. See note 4.

8. See note 4.

9. Southern Pacific Railroad Company employed large numbers of Mexican immigrants during the early years of the century.

10. Twelve of my twenty-nine Mexican American informants (41 percent) referred specifically to "upper-class" Mexican parents or ancestors. Others, while poor, identified with the upper class.

11. Eight of the forty-five informants (18 percent) claimed middle-class status as they were growing up. One, Robin Lemon, claimed upper-class status.

12. Steele, *The Content of Our Character*, relates the same sentiment: "Though my father was born poor, he achieved middle-class standing through much hard work and sacrifice (one of his favorite words) and by identifying fully with solid middle-class values—mainly hard work, family life, property ownership, and education for his children. . . . In his mind these were not so much values as laws of nature" (p. 98).

13. Robin Lemon grew up in New England as the daughter of wealthy parents. Her father, Meadowlark Lemon, was a star of the Harlem Globetrotters for many years. Lena Jones's parents both had middle-class jobs in New York City, where she grew up.

14. For example, see Tinto, *Leaving College;* Tinto, "Stages of Student Departure; Tinto, "Principles of Effective Retention."

15. For provocative discussions about some of the problems with respect to social Greek letter organizations see Ackerman, "The Survival of Greek Life"; Seitzinger, "Does Greek Life Belong?"; Goettsch, "Racism and Sexism in Greek Events"; and Horton, "Traditional Single-Sex Fraternities."

16. The Tohono O'odham people were formerly known as the Papago Indian Tribe. The Tohono O'odham reservation is just west of Tucson.

17. See note 4 in chapter 2.

18. Other writers disagree with this. For example, see Rooney, "Minority Students' Involvement in Minority Student Organizations." For another point of view see Babbitt and others, "Organizational Alienation among Black College Students"; Babbitt's team found that there was "less alienation"

among black students who associated with a small urban center than those attending a large urban university.

19. Some investigators feel that university administrators give themselves too much credit for the "growth" of undergraduates as a result of "adult-sponsored" and supervised activity. For an excellent discussion of this topic see Moffatt, "College Life."

20. See note 2 in chapter 1.

21. The national Catholic college student organization.

22. This thought is not original. Freeman, in "Racism, Rights and the Quest" writes, "Except when it is called to their attention, the whites in such a group do not pause to reflect on, or even notice, their own 'whiteness,' experiencing themselves instead as 'people in a room' with other people who are 'not white.' For the nonwhite, there is no chance to ignore the difference, because the nonwhite is always being experienced as 'other'" (p. 357). Many critical race theorists point this out, especially Williams in her autobiographical book, *The Alchemy of Race and Rights*.

23. William A. Mathews graduated from the University of Arizona in 1937.

24. George Miller completed his undergraduate degree in 1947 and a master's in education in 1953. He is currently the mayor of Tucson.

25. James Corbett Jr. graduated from the University of Arizona in 1947. He has served in many political positions, including mayor of Tucson.

26. See note 2 in chapter 1.

27. For two discussions about interracial dating, see Todd et al., "Attitudes Toward Interracial Dating"; and Davis, "Interracial Dating and Marriage Preferences."

28. See Yess, "The Influence of Marriage." Yess claims that marital status is an important predictor of community college success.

29. See Hood, *Men, Work, and Family*.

30. See note 28.

31. See note 29.

32. Statistics about minority student enrollment were not kept during this time period. McCray may have overestimated. A search of the 1960 University of Arizona yearbook revealed photos of only sixteen African American men and no African American women. Yearbook photos were not required. The African American fraternity, Kappa Alpha Psi, claimed seventeen members. The full-time student population for the 1959–60 first semester was 9,927 ("A Statistical Report," University of Arizona).

33. See note 2 in chapter 1.

34. McKale Center is the University of Arizona's basketball arena. Other teams, such as volleyball, use the basketball court for practice.

35. See Klafs and Lyon, *The Female Athlete*.

36. This feeling of cultural alienation should not be underestimated. For example, Weis quotes one of her informants in *Between Two Worlds* who suggests that someone must learn the dominant culture as if they "were some-

one from France coming here and having to learn to speak English" (p. 120). Also see Kempner, "Understanding Cultural Conflict."

37. Salomón Baldenegro entered the University of Arizona in 1965. Statistics of students by ethnicity were not kept at that time. His estimate is probably reasonably accurate. During the 1963–64 school year, the university enrolled 17,300 students for its first semester ("A Statistical Report," University of Arizona).,

38. The term "Chicano" itself is controversial and laden with political implications. The term generally refers to southwestern Mexican Americans as distinguished from other Americans of Hispanic heritage such as Cuban or Salvadoran Americans or Puerto Ricans. There are several theories about the origin of the term. One theory is that the term Chicano derives from the Mexican Indian way of saying *mexicano*. In their dialects the "x" is pronounced as "ch." Another theory is that it is a combination of CHIhuahua and mexiCANO and originated in south Texas. For some the term has nationalistic and cultural meaning. Many Mexican Americans reject the term as not representative of their political philosophies, preferring to refer to themselves as either Mexican Americans, Hispanics, or Americans of Mexican descent.

39. See note 2 in chapter 1.

40. Salpointe Catholic High School, Tucson.

41. Pueblo High School is located on Tucson's predominantly poor and Hispanic south side.

42. Tucson High School, Tucson.

43. Movimiento Estudiantil Chicano de Aztlan, a national movement made up of Mexican American students concerned with educational issues regarding Hispanics. See Martinez, "El Movimiento Estudiantil."

44. See note 41.

45. The New Start Summer Bridge Program grew out of the efforts of mainly Chicano activists and sympathetic faculty members during the late 1960s and early 1970s. Today it is a full program that offers "students an opportunity to become better prepared to meet the challenges awaiting them and to help ease the transition to the college environment" (*University of Arizona Record: 1993–94 General Catalog*).

46. See note 45.

47. All worked at least part time. Some received GI Bill support, athletic scholarships, or help from parents or spouses. For additional discussion on the effect of working on college students see Stern, "Paid Employment Among U.S. College Students"; Curtis, "To Work or Not to Work"; and Ehrenberg, "Employment While in College."

48. See note 47.

49. This opinion is shared by some contemporary conservative minority commentators. See note 4 in chapter 2.

50. Bell, *And We Are Not Saved,* has a lively discussion about this topic where he has Geneva Crenshaw say, "I don't care who agrees with me. . . .

Those conservatives are right about the need for blacks to get into jobs and off welfare" (p. 122).

51. See note 47.

52. Richard A. Harvill was president of the University of Arizona between 1951 and 1971.

53. See Maldonado, "Today's Chicano Refutes the Stereotype"; Rosenberg, *Stereotype and Tradition;* and Cross, "The Counselor, the Mexican American."

54. See note 47.

CHAPTER 4

1. January Esquivel completed her bachelor's degree in media arts at the University of Arizona in 1993.

2. For discussions about the diversity movement see Astin, "Diversity and Multiculturalism on Campus"; Astin, "Forging the Ties that Bind"; Ogbu, "Understanding Cultural Diversity and Learning"; and Wiley, "Educator Stresses Role of Cultural Centers."

3. Excerpt from "Poem for the Young White Man Who Asked Me How I, An Intelligent, Well-Read Person Could Believe in the War Between Races" from EMPLUMADA, by Lorna Dee Cervantes, © 1981. Reprinted by permission of the University of Pittsburgh Press.

4. See Leslie and Brinkman, *The Economic Value of Higher Education.* By analyzing aggregate data and computing internal rates of return for different segments, the authors concluded that—from a purely financial point of view—higher education is an excellent investment for most individuals. Most of the persons whom I interviewed acknowledged that the material benefits they enjoyed had resulted partly from their college education, but they preferred to dwell on their personal intellectual enrichment instead.

5. At the time Arizona required segregated schools for African American students in elementary schools and permitted segregation in the high schools. Arizona Revised Statutes Section 54-416 read: "The Board (of Trustees) . . . shall segregate pupils of the African race from pupils of the Caucasian race in all schools other than high schools, and provide all accommodations made necessary by such segregation." See *Close the Breach,* a 1949 pamphlet by the Arizona Council for Civic Unity.

6. At the time, the Pioneer Hotel in downtown Tucson was the community's largest and most luxurious hotel.

7. Fred Enke was a legendary basketball coach at the University of Arizona from 1925 until 1960. He coached golf until his retirement in 1966.

8. During the 1993-94 school year the University, under the category "Budgeted Instructional Faculty" claimed eighteen "Black-Non Hispanic" faculty members, 1.1 percent of the 1,587 total for "Budgeted Instructional Faculty" (*University of Arizona Factbook*).

9. Texas Tech University, Lubbock, Texas.

10. In his interview, Hadie reported that this game took place in 1951. My research shows that the game actually took place on January 17, 1954. I had the opportunity to speak with several of Redd's white teammates who recounted similar stories. They admitted that, at the time, it did not occur to them to protest or complain. Arizona won the January 17th game, 77-68. Redd led his team in scoring with eighteen points.

11. Now the University of Texas at El Paso.

12. The Stone Avenue underpass runs under a railroad track and connects Tucson's downtown area to the neighborhoods just north.

13. Bell, *And We Are Not Saved,* pp. 190–191.

14. "Bear Down" Gym is where basketball was played during that time.

15. In "Race Consciousness," Barnes describes what she calls the pervasive message "that we do not truly belong." She says this "other" consciousness "is reinforced across the generations in our familial and community interactions." Sharing much the same idea that Ernie is in this statement, Barnes writes, "Many of us remember when we first realized that we were black, and that discovery had a more profound impact than every other thereafter."

16. p. 6.

17. *La Llorona* (The Weeping Woman) is the most famous of many folk stories that seem to be part of every Mexican American neighborhood in the U.S. *El Vaquero* is another.

18. *The Alchemy of Race and Rights,* p. 113.

19. Bell, *Faces at the Bottom of the Well,* p. 43.

20. Allan Bakke, a white applicant to the University of California Medical School, sued when he was denied a spot, alleging reverse discrimination. In a 1978 ruling, the U.S. Circuit Court held in his favor (Regents of California v. Bakke, 438 U.S.). The litigation, and eventually the ruling, had a chilling effect on the admissions process with respect to minorities. See Astin, *Admitting and Assisting Students After Bakke;* and Haro and Gomez-Quinones, *The Bakke Decision.*

21. Williams, *The Alchemy of Race and Rights,* suggests that the objections of some people to affirmative action go deeper than perhaps seeing a friend being denied a slot in law school. She says, "Affirmative action challenges many people who believe in the truism that this is a free country. For people who don't believe that there is such a thing as institutional racism, statements alleging oppression sound like personal attacks, declarations of war" (p. 102).

22. In "Community Ties and Law School Faculty Hiring," Lopez suggests that identity with a minority community is an important factor to consider when attempting to seek a less homogenous faculty (in this case). Simply having black skin or a Hispanic last name, in his view, does not automatically serve the purpose. Lopez strongly advocates the importance of both "the minority perspective" and of role models, but he points out that "a single role model cannot suffice for any community or individual . . . The complexity of

minority communities requires not one but many representative role models" (p. 112).

23. The notion that successful minorities should serve as role models is not necessarily universally accepted. For an interesting argument suggesting that "role models" tend to serve the dominant classes to a greater degree than members of the minority or subordinate community from which the success-ful individual came, see Delgado, "Affirmative Action as a Majoritarian Device"; and Scarbecz, *Parental Influence.*

24. Delgado presents a fascinating discussion about the state of legal education in "Rodrigo's Fifth Chronicle."

25. In "Racism, Rights and the Quest for Equality," Freeman said starkly, "Equality of opportunity is a myth that does not permit one to notice the un-American reality of a pervasive and recurring class structure" (p. 363). In "The 'Official' Ideology of Higher Education," Slaughter describes the "ways in which ideas are used to legitimate structures of privilege and power and, often inadvertently, to mask inequities and injustices." Also see Weis, *Issues in Education;* Weis, *Between Two Worlds;* Macleod, *Ain't No Makin' It;* Jencks and Reisman, "Social Stratification"; Jencks, *Who Gets Ahead?*

26. For an excellent discussion of the difficulty in a law school environ-ment, see Bell, *Confronting Authority.* For a quantitative look at how little movement between classes has actually taken place, especially from an African American perspective, see Hacker, *Two Nations.* Hacker uses quan-titative data over the course of five decades to show that the economic and social status of African Americans relative to Anglos has not improved and in some cases has fallen. He shows that the many African American success stories that we hear and read about are exceptions and do not accurately reflect the true picture of continuing patterns of poverty, discrimination, and lack of opportunity for America's blacks.

27. Bell, *Faces at the Bottom of the Well,* p. xi.

CHAPTER 5

1. Williams, *The Alchemy of Race and Rights,* pp. 44–51, discusses this issue in her now famous story about being denied entry into a Benetton store in New York City.

2. I do not have rigorous definitions for either "activism" or "resistance," therefore, the twenty-two individuals in my sample whom I include in this category exhibited a wide range of behavior, from personal confrontation (Andrews) to simply leaving an untenable situation (Lander), to actual "to the streets" protest (Baldenegro and Bowens). The factor, for me, was not the specific behavior or action but whether the activism or resistance was a defining part of the university lives of my informants. See, for example, the discussion about Los Universitarios in chapter 4.

3. Stewart L. Udall completed his law degree at the University of Arizona in 1948. He served in Congress and under President Kennedy as Secretary of the Interior.

4. See chapter 3, note 25.

5. F. T. ("Limey") Gibbings graduated from the University of Arizona in 1926.

6. See chapter 1, note 2. The term "gringa" is generally used to refer to Anglo American women. At the time, it was not necessarily considered a negative term, but certainly did signify "other."

7. The National Council of La Raza still exists, promotes Chicano community activism, and publishes papers and books relating to the improvement of the Mexican American condition in the United States.

8. See Rosen, "The Development of the Chicano Movement."

9. See Fogelson, *The Los Angeles Riots.*

10. Salpointe Catholic High School, Tucson.

11. See chapter 3, note 43.

12. See note 22 in chapter 2. Also see Gonzalez, "Positive and Negative Effects of Chicano Militancy on the Education of the Mexican American," in which she examines Chicano organizations in five southwestern states with respect to their philosophies on activism affecting education.

13. Cholla High School is located on Tucson's far west side. At the time it was one of Tucson's newest high schools.

14. See chapter 3, note 52.

15. Marana is a small farming community about thirty miles north of Tucson.

16. See chapter 3, note 43.

17. See chapter 3, note 43.

18. See chapter 3, note 38.

19. Bell cites economist Matthew Goldberg in suggesting that "racial nepotism" rather than "racial animus" is the "major motivation for much of the discrimination blacks experience." Bell, *Faces at the Bottom of the Well,* p. 56.

20. Clifford M. Lytle is a professor of political science at the University of Arizona.

21. John P. Schaefer was University of Arizona President between 1971 and 1982.

22. See note 5.

23. The Arizona Constitution required Frank to wait until his twenty-fifth birthday to be sworn in as a state senator.

24. Rubin Salter completed his undergraduate degree in 1956 and his law degree in 1964 at the University of Arizona.

25. Alton N. Sparks graduated from the University of Arizona in 1961.

26. See chapter 3, note 52.

27. Bear Down Gym was where intercollegiate basketball games were held at the time.

28. Marvin D. ("Swede") Johnson was vice president for university relations.

29. John Heard graduated from the University of Arizona in 1970.

30. Gale A. Dean graduated from the University of Arizona in 1972.

31. Sylvia E. Goodwin completed her bachelor's degree in 1970 and her law degree in 1988, both at the University of Arizona.

32. Others have made this point. In "Racism, Rights and the Quest for Equality of Opportunity," Freeman put it this way: "If you get guns, they will come and kill you with theirs, and they have more of them" (p. 295).

33. League of United Latin American Citizens. See Márquez, *LULAC*.

34. See chapter 4 where Jones describes an incident during a football game at Arizona Stadium.

CHAPTER 6

1. The Civil Rights Act of 1964. See Loevy, *To End All Segregation*.

2. *University of Arizona Record: 1993–94,* pp. 33, 34.

3. See chapter 3, note 38.

4. Some critical race theorists and others would take issue with an individual who chooses to use the existence of "ethnic" or "special interest" clubs as evidence of social change. For example, in "Critical Race Theory," Torres writes, "to say that a cultural subgrouping is merely an interest group is to assume from the outset that the political expression of the group's cultural life captures the essence of the collectivity and defines any particular member of the group. Such a move, of course, protects the dominant cultural grouping from confronting the destabilizing 'other,' and forces the subordinate group to adopt the dominant group's definition of themselves if they wish to share in the distribution of social goods" (p. 999).

5. See chapter 3, note 45.

6. Manual T. Pacheco is president of the University of Arizona.

7. Steele (*The Content of Our Character*) questions whether techniques such as the establishment of "centers" and the like address the problem when he points out, "At the university where I currently teach, the dropout rate for black students is 72 percent, despite the presence of several academic support programs, a counseling center with black counselors, an Afro-American studies department, black faculty, administrators, and staff, a general education curriculum that emphasizes 'cultural pluralism,' an Educational Opportunities Program, a mentor program, a black faculty and staff association, and an administration and faculty that often announce the need for more black students" (pp. 138–39). Also see chapter 5, note 2.

8. See chapter 2, note 4.

9. Bell's most recent book is, in some senses, a response to this question, one which he has been asked since he began to be identified as the father of the critical race theory movement. See *Confronting Authority*.

10. For an incisive critique of critical race theory and Bell, Matsuda, and Delgado specifically, see Kennedy, "Racial Critiques of Legal Academia," p. 1745. For a critique from a left point of view of the critical legal studies, in many ways the parent of the critical race theory movement, see West, "Brendan Brown Lecture."

11. Matsuda, *Words that Wound*, p. 6.

12. See chapter 2, notes 1, 5, and 8.

13. See chapter 4, note 23.

14. Williams, *The Alchemy of Race and Rights: Diary of a Law Professor,* relates critical race theory to the problem of class in America: "I take as a given two counterfacts: that in the United States we subsidize the wealthy in all kinds of ways, and we do so in a way that directly injures the poor; and that neither the state of indigency nor the state of wealth is necessarily or even frequently the result of freely exercised choice" (p. 28).

15. See chapter 4, note 23.

16. Bell, in *And We Are Not Saved,* makes this point in his chapter entitled, "The Benefits to Whites of Civil Rights Litigation," when he has one of his characters state, "They know, or should know, that in a society where money is fundamental, equality that does not include economic equality is not equality at all" (p. 53). Bell repeats the point in *Faces at the Bottom of the Well:* "In our battles with racism, we need less discussion of ethics and more discussion of economics—much more. Ideals must not be allowed to obscure the blacks' real position in the socioeconomic realm, which happens to be the real indicator of power in this country" (p. 98).

17. Freeman, in "Racism, Rights and the Quest for Equality," discusses the notion of "cultural capital" which is "already more or less possessed by the powerful." He suggests that "in such a 'meritocracy,' historical access to and acquisition of such cultural capital may be much more important than wealth itself" (p. 384). Bell, in *Confronting Authority,* cited Dr. Martin Luther King Jr. to make this point: "Toward the end of his life, Dr. King came to realize that the civil rights gains he had worked to achieve would be meaningless without deeper social and, in particular, economic reform" (p. 170, note 4).

18. Steele, in *The Content of Our Character,* discusses the conflicts first-generation middle-class minorities face. Responding to critics who define the situation of African Americans solely in terms of race, he says, "When I honestly look at my life and the lives of many other middle-class blacks I know, I can see that race never fully explained our situation in American society. Black though I may be, it is impossible for me to sit in my single-family house with two cars in the driveway and a swing set in the backyard and not see the role class has played in my life" (p. 94).

Bibliography

Ackerman, R. "The Survival of Greek Life: Concerns and Solutions." *NASPA Journal* 28(1): (Fall 1990).

Aleinikoff, A. T. "A Case for Race-Consciousness." *Columbia Law Review* 91:1060 (1991).

Altbach, P. G., and K. Lomotey, eds. *The Racial Crisis in American Higher Education*. Albany: State University of New York Press, 1991.

Anderson, B. "Hidden Hurdles that Block the Road to College." *Times Educational Supplement* 3882:80 (November 23, 1990).

Ansley, T. N. "Relationship of Elementary and Secondary School Achievement Test Scores to College Performance." *Educational and Psychological Measurement* 43(4):1103–1112 (Winter 1983).

Arizona Council for Civic Unity. *Close the Breach: A Study of School Segregation in Arizona*. Tucson: University of Arizona Special Collections, 1949.

Arnot, M. "Male Hegemony, Social Class and Women's Education." *Journal of Education* 164(1):64–89 (1982).

Astin, A. W. "The Myth of Equal Access." *Educational Research and Methods* 9(1):6–8 (1976).

Astin, A. W. *Admitting and Assisting Students After Bakke*. San Francisco: Jossey-Bass, 1978.

Astin, A. W. *The Black Undergraduate: Current Status and Trends in the Characteristics of Freshmen*. Los Angeles: Higher Education Research Institute, Graduate School of Education, University of California, Los Angeles, 1990.

Astin, A. W. "Diversity and Multiculturalism on Campus: How Are Students Affected?" *Change* 25(2):44–49 (March/April 1993a).

Astin, A. W. "Forging the Ties that Bind: The Dilemma of the Modern University." *College Board Review* 165:12–15, 26–27 (Winter 1993b).

Astin, A. W., E. L. Day, and W. S. Korn. *The American Freshman: Twenty-Five Year Trends, 1966–1990*. Los Angeles: Higher Education Research Institute, Graduate School of Education, University of California, Los Angeles, 1991.

Attinasi, L. C., Jr. "Getting in: Mexican Americans' Perceptions of University Attendance and the Implications for Freshman Year Persistence." *Journal of Higher Education* 60(3):247–277 (May–June 1989).

Attinasi, L. C., Jr. "Rethinking the Study of the Outcomes of College Attendance." *Journal of College Student Development* 33(1):61–70 (January 1992).

Babbitt, C. E., H. J. Burbach, and Thompson, M. A., III. "Organizational Alienation Among Black College Students: A Comparison of Three

Educational Settings." *Journal of College Student Personnel* 16(1):53–56 (January 1975).

Barnes, R. D. "Race Consciousness: The Thematic Content of Racial Distinctiveness in Critical Race Scholarship." *Harvard Law Review* 103:1866–1867 (1990).

Bean, J. P. "Dropouts and Turnover: The Synthesis and Test of a Causal Model of Student Attrition." *Research in Higher Education* 12:155–187 (1980).

Bean, J. P. "Student Attrition, Intentions, and Confidence: Interaction Effects in a Path Model." *Research in Higher Education* 17:291–320 (1982).

Bean, J. P. "The Application of a Model of Turnover in Work Organizations to the Student Attrition Process." *Review of Higher Education* 6:129–148 (1983).

Bean, J. P. "Interaction Effects Based on Class Level in an Explanatory Model of College Student Dropout Syndrome." *American Educational Research Journal* 22:35–64 (1985).

Bean, J. P., and B. S. Metzner. "The Synthesis of a Theoretical Model of Student Attrition." Paper presented at the annual meeting of the American Educational Research Association (ERIC Document Reproduction Service No. ED 20244), April 1981.

Bean, J. P., and B. S. Metzner. "A Conceptual Model of Nontraditional Undergraduate Student Attrition." *Review of Educational Research* 55:485–540 (1985).

Bell, D. A., Jr. *And We Are Not Saved: The Elusive Quest for Racial Justice.* New York: Basic, 1987.

Bell, D. A., Jr. *Faces at the Bottom of the Well: The Permanence of Racism.* New York: Basic, 1992.

Bell, D. A., Jr. *Confronting Authority: Reflections of an Ardent Protester.* Boston: Beacon, 1994.

Bernstein, B. "Social Class, Language, and Socialization." In *Power and Ideology in Education,* edited by J. Karabel and A. H. Halsey. New York: Oxford University Press, 1977.

Bierstedt, R. "The Sociology of Majorities." *American Sociological Review* 13: (1948).

Blea, I. I. 1992. *La Chicana and the Intersection of Race, Class, and Gender.* New York: Praeger, 1992.

Bolman, L. G., and T. Deal. *Modern Approaches to Understanding and Managing Organizations.* San Francisco: Jossey-Bass, 1989.

Bourdieu, P. "Cultural Reproduction and Social Reproduction." In *Power and Ideology in Education,* edited by J. Karabel and A. H. Halsey. New York: Oxford University Press, 1977.

Bowles, S., and H. Gintis. *Schooling in Capitalist America.* New York: Basic, 1976.

Brown v Board of Education, 347 U.S. 483 (1954).

Cabrera, C., and E. Howard. *Oral History Project: Literature Review and Recommendations for Research.* Unpublished manuscript, 1988.

Carmichael, S., and C. V. Hamilton. *Black Power: The Politics of Black Libera-tion in America.* New York: Vintage, 1967.

Carter, S. L. *Reflections of an Affirmative Action Baby.* New York: United States Basic Books, Harper Collins, 1991.

Castaneda, M. B., A. Nora, and D. Hengstler. "The Convergence Between Two Theories of College Persistence." *Journal of Higher Education* 63(2): (1992).

Christie, N. G., and S. M. Dinham. "Institutional and External Influences on Social Integration in the Freshman Year." *Journal of Higher Education* 62(4):412–436 (1991).

Colon, A. "Race Relations on Campus: An Administrative Perspective." In *The Racial Crisis in American Higher Education,* edited by P. G. Altbach and K. Lomotey. Albany: State University of New York Press, 1991.

Commins, N. L. "Parents and Public Schools: The Experiences of Four Mexi-can Immigrant Families." *Equity and Choice* 8(2):40–45 (Winter 1992).

Cordova, T. *Chicana Voices: Intersections of Class, Race, and Gender.* Austin: University of Texas, Center for Mexican American Studies, 1986.

"The Costs of Being Black." *Research News* 38: (1987).

Crenshaw, K. W. "Foreword: Toward a Race-Conscious Pedagogy in Legal Education." *National Black Law Journal* 11:1 (1989).

Cross, W. C. "The Counselor, the Mexican American and the Stereotype." *Elementary School Guidance and Counseling* 6(1):27–31 (October 1971).

Culp, J. M., Jr. "Autobiography and Legal Scholarship and Teaching: Finding the Me in the Legal Academy." *Virginia Law Review* 77:539 (1991).

Curtis, G. "To Work or Not to Work: That Is the Question." *Journal of Student Financial Aid* 21(3):16–26 (Fall 1991).

Damashek, B., M. Newman, P. Cooper, and M. Fauss. *Quilters.* Vocal Score. New York: Dramatists Play Service, 1986.

Darity, W. A., Jr. "The Human Capital Approach to Black-White Earnings Inequality: Some Unsettled Questions." *Journal of Human Resources* 17:90–98 (1982).

Davis, E. G. "Interracial Dating and Marriage Preferences Among Blacks, Chicanos and Anglos." Paper presented at the annual meeting of the Southwestern Sociological Association, San Antonio, Texas. (ERIC Document Reproduction Service No. ED 104 609), March 27, 1975.

Davis, J. S. "Parents: The Hidden Resource." *College Board Review* 106:24–29 (Winter 1977–1978).

Davis, J. S. "Athletics As Academic Motivation for the Inner City Boy." *Journal of Health Physical Education Recreation* 43(2):40–41 (Winter 1977–1978).

Delgado, R. "The Imperial Scholar: Reflections on a Review of Civil Rights Literature." *University of Pennsylvania Law Review* 132:561 (1984).

Delgado, R. "Critical Legal Studies and the Realities of Race: Does the Funda-mental Contradiction Have a Corollary?" *Harvard Civil Rights–Civil Liberties Law Review* 23:407 (1988).

Delgado, R. "Storytelling for Oppositionists and Others: A Plea for Narrative."
Michigan Law Review 87:2411 (1989).

Delgado, R. "Affirmative Action As a Majoritarian Device: Or, Do You Really
Want to Be a Role Model?" *Michigan Law Review* 89:1222 (1991).

Delgado, R. "Enormous Anomaly? Left-Right Parallels in Recent Writing
About Race." *Columbia Law Review* 91:1547 (1991).

Delgado, R. "The Imperial Scholar Revisited: How to Marginalize Outsider
Writing, Ten Years Later." *University of Pennsylvania Law Review* 132:561
(1992).

Delgado, R. "Rodrigo's Second Chronicle: The Economics and Politics of
Race." *Michigan Law Review* 91:1183 (May 1993).

Delgado, R. "Rodrigo's Third Chronicle: Care, Competition, and the Redemp-
tive Tragedy of Race." *California Law Review* 387 (1993).

Delgado, R. "Rodrigo's Fifth Chronicle: Civitas, Civil Wrongs, and the Politics
of Denial." *Stanford Law Review* 45:1581 (July 1993).

Delgado, R., and J. Stefanic. "Critical Race Theory: An Annotated Bibliog-
raphy." *Virginia Law Review* 79:461 (1993).

The Desert. Tucson: Associated Students of the University of Arizona, 1934.

The Desert. Tucson: Associated Students of the University of Arizona, 1946.

The Desert. Tucson: Associated Students of the University of Arizona, 1954.

The Desert. Tucson: Associated Students of the University of Arizona, 1960.

Dilanian, S. M. *The Influence of Peer Group Pressure Upon Adolescents'
Learning.* (ERIC Document Reproduction Service No. ED 198 411), January
1980.

Dubois, W. E. B. *The Souls of Black Folk: Essays and Sketches.* New York:
Johnson Reprint [1903], 1968.

Durkheim, E. *Suicide,* translated by J. A. Spaulding and G. Simpson. Glencoe,
Ill.: Free Press, [1897], 1951.

Ehrenberg, R. G. "Employment While in College: Academic Achievement and
Postcollege Outcomes." *Journal of Human Resources* 22(1):1–23 (Winter
1987).

Ferlinghetti, L. *A Coney Island of the Mind.* New York: New Directions, 1958.

Fogelson, R. M. *The Los Angeles Riots.* Mass Violence in America Series. New
York: Arno Press, 1969.

Foley, D. E. "Reconsidering Anthropological Explanations of Ethnic School
Failure." *Anthropology and Education Quarterly* 22:60–86 (1991).

Fordham, S., and J. U. Ogbu. "Black Students' School Success: Coping With
the Burden of 'Acting White.'" *The Urban Review* 18(3):176–206 (1986).

Frazier, E. F. *The Negro in the United States.* Rev. ed. New York: Macmillan,
1957.

Freeman, A. "Racism, Rights and the Quest for Equality of Opportunity: A
Critical Legal Essay." *Harvard Civil Rights–Civil Liberties Law Review*
23:295 (1988).

Giroux, H. A. *Theory and Resistance in Education.* London: Heinemann, 1983.

Goettsch, J. M. "Racism and Sexism in Greek Events: A Call for Sensitivity." *NASPA Journal* 28(1):65–70 (Fall 1990).

Goldwater, B. M. *The Conscience of a Conservative.* Shepherdsville, Kentucky: Victor, 1960.

Gonzalez, N. L. "Positive and Negative Effects of Chicano Militancy on the Education of the Mexican American." (ERIC Document Reproduction Service No. ED 061004), January 1970.

Gordon, L., and A. Gordon. *American Chronicle: Six Decades in American Life, 1920–1980.* New York: Atheneum, 1987.

Hacker, A. *Two Nations: Black and White, Separate, Hostile, Unequal.* New York: Scribners, 1992.

Hamlish, M., and E. Kleban. *A Chorus Line.* Vocal Score. New York: E. H. Morris.

Hammonds, E. "Clarence Thomas and the Academy." In *Beyond a Dream Deferred: Multicultural Education and the Politics of Excellence,* edited by B. W. Thompson and S. Tyagi, 66–79. Minneapolis: University of Minnesota Press, 1993.

Haro, C. M., and J. Gomez-Quinones. *The Bakke Decision: The Question of Chicano Access to Higher Education.* Los Angeles: University of California, Chicano Studies Center, 1977.

Hawkins, B. B. "Pre-College Counselors Challenged for Misadvising Minorities: Full Array of Options Not Always Explored." *Black Issues in Higher Education* 10(11):14–15 (July 29, 1993).

Hawthorne, N. *The Scarlet Letter.* Boston: Houghton Mifflin, 1878.

Hayes, J., and V. Trego Hill. *La Llorona—The Weeping Woman: An Hispanic Legend.* El Paso: Cinco Puntos, 1987.

Henson, J. W. "The Minority Pipeline: Minorities at Different Educational Transition Points." *New Directions for Higher Education* 6(3):41–46 (1978).

Herrnstein, R. J., and C. A. Murray. *The Bell Curve: Intelligence and Class Structure in American Life.* New York: Free Press, 1994.

Holland, D. C., and M. A. Eisenhart. *Educated in Romance: Women, Achievement, and College Culture.* Chicago: University of Chicago Press, 1990.

Hood, J. C. *Men, Work, and Family. Research on Men and Masculinities.* Series 4. Newbury Park, Calif.: Sage, 1993.

Horton, N. S. "Traditional Single-Sex Fraternities on College Campuses: Will They Survive in the 1990s?" *Journal of College and University Law* 18(4) 418–482 (Spring 1992).

Hughes, L. *The Ways of White Folks.* New York: Knopf, 1969.

Ives, E. D. *The Tape Recorded Interview: A Manual for Field Workers in Folklore and Oral History.* Knoxville: University of Tennessee Press, 1987.

Jaynes, G. D., and R. M. Williams, eds. *A Common Destiny: Blacks and American Society.* Washington, D.C.: National Academy Press, 1989.

Jencks, C. *Inequality: A Reassessment of the Effect of Family and Schooling in America.* New York: Basic, 1972.

Jencks, C. *Who Gets Ahead? The Determinants of Economic Success in America.* New York: Basic, 1979.

Jencks, C., and D. Reisman. "Social Stratification and Mass Higher Education." In *The Academic Revolution.* Chicago: University of Chicago Press, 1977.

Karabel, H., and T. H. Halsey. *Education and Inequality.* New York: Oxford University Press, 1977.

Karabel, J. "Social Class, Academic Ability, and College Quality." *Social Forces* 53(3):381–398 (1975).

Karen, D. "The Politics of Class, Race and Gender: Access to Higher Education in the United States, 1960–1986." *American Journal of Education* 99(2): 208–237 (February 1994).

Kelly, G. P., and A. Nihlen. "Schooling and the Reproduction of Patriarchy: Unequal Workloads, Unequal Rewards." In *Cultural and Economic Reproduction in American Education: Essays in Class, Ideology and the State,* edited by M. Apple, 162–180. Boston: Routledge and Kegan Paul, 1982.

Kempner, K. "Understanding Cultural Conflict." In *Culture and Ideology in Higher Education: Advancing a Critical Agenda,* edited by W. G. Tierney, 129–150. New York: Praeger, 1991.

Kennedy, "Racial Critiques of Legal Academia." *Harvard Law Review* 102:1745 (1989).

King, M. L. *The Role of the Behavioral Scientist in the Civil Rights Movement.* Initial address to the American Psychological Association, 1967.

Klafs, C. E., and J. M. Lyon. *The Female Athlete: Conditioning, Competition, and Culture.* St. Louis: Mosby, 1973.

Kluegel, J. R., and E. R. Smith. "Whites' Beliefs About Black Opportunity." *American Sociological Review* 47:518–532 (1982).

Leslie, L., and P. Brinkman. *The Economic Value of Higher Education.* New York: Macmillan, 1988.

Loevy, R. D. *To End All Segregation: The Politics of the Passage of the Civil Rights Act of 1964.* Lanham, Md.: University Press of America, 1990.

Lofland, J., and L. Lofland. *Analyzing Social Settings: A Guide to Qualitative Observation and Analysis.* Belmont, Calif.: Wadsworth, 1984.

London, H. B. "Transformations: Cultural Challenges Faced by First-Generation Students." *New Directions for Community Colleges* 20(4):5–11 (Winter 1992).

Lopez, I. H. "Community Ties, Race, and Faculty Hiring: The Case for Professors Who Don't Think White." *Reconstruction* 1(3):46 (1991).

Lopez, I. H. "Community Ties and Law School Faculty Hiring." In *Beyond a Dream Deferred: Multicultural Education and the Politics of Excellence,* edited by B. W. Thompson and S. Tyagi, 100–130. Minneapolis: University of Minnesota Press, 1993.

Lyons, G. *Tales the People Tell in Mexico.* New York: J. Messner, 1972.

MacDermott, K. G., and others. "The Influence of Parental Education Level on College Choice." *Journal of College Admissions* 115:3–10 (Spring 1987).

Macleod, J. *Ain't No Makin' It: Leveled Aspirations in a Low-Income Neighborhood.* Boulder, Colo.: Westview, 1987.

Malcolm X. *Malcolm X on Afro-American History.* New York: Merit, 1967.

Maldonado, B. M. "Today's Chicano Refutes the Stereotype." *College Student Journal* 11(2):146–151 (Summer 1977).

Márquez, B. *LULAC: The Evolution of a Mexican American Political Organization.* Austin: University of Texas Press, 1993.

Martinez, D. R. "El Movimiento Estudiantil: From the Sixties to the Seventies." *Agenda* 8(3):19–21 (1978).

Mathews, C. J. *A Bull in a China Shop: A Comedy in Two Acts.* Boston: W. H. Baker, 1989.

Matsuda, M. J., C. R. Lawrence III, R. Delgado, and K. W. Crenshaw. *Words That Wound: Critical Race Theory, Assaultive Speech, and the First Amendment.* Boulder, Colo.: Westview, 1993.

Merton, R. K. "Discrimination and the American Creed." In *Discrimination and the National Welfare,* edited by R. Maciver. New York: Institute for Religious and Social Studies. Harper and Row, 1949.

Modell, J., M. Goulden, and S. Magnusson. "World War II in the Lives of Black Americans: Some Findings and an Interpretation." *Journal of American History* 76(2):383 (December 1989).

Moffatt, M. "College Life: Undergraduate Culture and Higher Education." *Journal of Higher Education* 62(1) (January/February 1991).

Moore, D. "The Importance of Different Home-Leaving Strategies to Late Adolescents." *Adolescence* 18(70):413–416 (Summer 1983).

Myers, G. *History of Bigotry in the United States.* New York: Random House, 1943.

Myrdal, G., and R. M. E. Sterner. *An American Dilemma: The Negro Problem and Modern Democracy.* New York: Harper and Brothers, 1944.

Ogbu, J. U. *Minority Education and Caste: The American System in Cross-Cultural Perspective.* New York: Academic, 1978.

Ogbu, J. U. "Schooling in the Inner City." *Society* (November/December 1983).

Ogbu, J. U. "Variability in Minority School Performance: A Problem in Search of an Explanation." *Anthropology and Education Quarterly* 18 (1987).

Ogbu, J. U. "Understanding Cultural Diversity and Learning." *Educational Researcher* 21(8):5–14, 24 (November 1992).

Pang, O. P. "Ethnic Prejudice: Still Alive and Hurtful." *Harvard Educational Review* 58(3): (August 1988).

Parker, W. M. "An Awareness Experience: Toward Counseling Minorities." *Counselor Education and Supervision* 18(4):312–317 (June 1979).

Plummer, K. *Documents of Life: An Introduction to the Problems and Literature of a Humanistic Method.* London: George, Allen and Unwin, 1983.

Porter, E. H. *Pollyanna.* Boston: L. C. Page, 1913.

Prett, P. A. "First Generation College Students: Are They at Greater Risk for Attrition Than Their Peers?" *Research in Rural Education* 6(2):31–34 (1989).

Ransford, E. H. *Race and Class in American Society: Black, Latino, Anglo.* Rev. ed. Rochester, Vt: Schenkman, 1994.

R.A.V. v St. Paul, L. Ed 2d 305 at 326 (1992).

Reyes, M., and J. J. Halcon. "Practices of the Academy: Barriers to Access for Chicano Academics." In *The Racial Crisis in American Higher Education,* edited by P. G. Altbach and K. Lomotey. Albany: State University of New York Press, 1991.

Rhoades, G. *Organizational Theory.* Unpublished instructional material, University of Arizona, 1985.

Rhoades, G. "Calling on the Past: The Quest for the Collegiate Ideal." *Journal of Higher Education* 61(5): (September/October 1990).

Richardson, R. C., Jr. "Helping First-Generation Minority Students Achieve Degrees." *New Directions for Community Colleges* 20(4):29–43 (Winter 1992).

Rodriguez, R. *Hunger for Memory: The Education of Richard Rodriguez.* New York: Bantam Books, 1982.

Rooney, G. D. "Minority Students' Involvement in Minority Student Organizations: An Exploratory Study." *Journal of College Student Personnel* 26(5):450–456 (September 1985).

Rosen, G. "The Development of the Chicano Movement in Los Angeles from 1967 to 1969." *Aztlan* 4(1):155–183 (Spring 1973).

Rosenberg, N. V. *Stereotype and Tradition: White Folklore About Blacks.* Ph.D. dissertation, Indiana University, 1970.

Scarbecz, M. *Parental Influence on the Educational Expectations of High School Students: A Role Identity Model.* Ph.D. dissertation, University of Arizona, 1991.

Schatzman, L., and A. Strauss. *Field Research: Strategies for a Natural Sociology.* Englewood Cliffs, N.J.: Prentice-Hall, 1973.

Schuman, H. "Sociological Racism." *Transaction* 7 (1969).

Schuman, H., C. Steeh, and L. Bobo. *Racial Attitudes in America: Trends and Interpretations.* Cambridge: Harvard University Press, 1985.

Sedlacek, W. E., and G. C. Brooks Jr. *Racism in American Education: A Model for Change.* Chicago: Nelson, 1976.

Seitzinger, J. A. "Does Greek Life Belong? Two Roads to Community. Creating a New Residential Life System. Setting New Goals for the Greek System." *Educational Record* 70(3–4):48–53 (Summer/Fall 1989).

Shoemaker, S. B. "Reasons Why the Technical Vocabulary of College Admissions Should be Taught to Parents and Students Beginning in Elementary School." Paper presented at the annual meeting of the National Association of College Admission Counselors, Washington, D.C. (ERIC Document Reproduction Service No. ED 278 903), October 5–8, 1986.

Slaughter, S. "The 'Official' Ideology of Higher Education: Ironies and Inconsistencies." In *Culture and Ideology in Higher Education,* edited by W. G. Tierney. New York: Praeger, 1991.

Smith, G. S. "Developing Career Cognizance, Goals and Choices in Minorities." *Journal of Non-White Concerns in Personnel and Guidance* 9(1):19–22 (October 1980).

Smitherman-Donaldson, G., and T. A. Van Dijk. *Discourse and Discrimination.* Detroit: Wayne State University Press, 1988.

Sowell, T. "Affirmative Action Reconsidered: Was It Necessary in Academia? Evaluative Studies." *American Enterprise Institute for Public Policy Research* 27 (1975).

Spady, W. "Dropouts from Higher Education: An Interdisciplinary Review and Synthesis." *Interchange* 1:64–85 (1971).

Spence, M. *Market Signaling.* Cambridge: Harvard University Press, 1975.

Spradley, J. P. *The Ethnographic Interview.* Chicago: Holt, Rinehart, and Winston, 1979.

Spradley, J. P., and D. W. McCurdy. *The Cultural Experience.* Chicago: Science Research Associates, 1972.

A Statistical Report of Finances, Enrollments, Programs, and Degrees, 1963–64. Tucson: University of Arizona, September 1964.

Steele, S. *The Content of Our Character: A New Vision of Race in America.* New York: St. Martin, 1990.

Steinbeck, J. *The Pearl.* New York: Viking, 1947.

Stern, D. "Paid Employment Among U.S. College Students: Trends, Effects, and Possible Causes." *Journal of Higher Education* 62(1): (January/February 1991).

Stewart, D. M. "Education, Race, and Class: A New Calculus for the 21st Century." *Journal of Negro Education* 62(2):113–124 (Spring 1993).

Sturtevant, W. C. "Studies in Ethnoscience." *American Anthropologist* 66(2):99–131 (1964).

Terenzini, P. T., L. I. Rendon, M. L. Upcraft, S. B. Millor, K. W. Allison, P. L. Gregg, and R. Jalomo. "The Transition to College: Diverse Students, Diverse Stories." *Research in Higher Education* 35(1):57–73 (1994).

Thomas, G. E. "Black Students in U.S. Graduate and Professional Schools in the 1980s: A National and Institutional Assessment." *Harvard Educational Review* 57(3):261–282 (August 1987).

Thurow, L. C. *Poverty and Discrimination.* Washington, D.C.: Brookings Institution, 1970.

Thurow, L. C. *Generating Inequality.* New York: Basic, 1975.

Tierney, W. G. "An Anthropological Analysis of Student Participation in College." *Journal of Higher Education* 63(6): (1992).

Tinto, V. "Dropout From Higher Education: A Theoretical Synthesis of Recent Research." *Review of Educational Research* 45:89–125 (1975).

Tinto, V. "Limits of Theory and Practice in Student Attrition." *Journal of Higher Education* 53(6): 1982.

Tinto, V. *Leaving College: Rethinking the Causes and Cures of Student Attrition.* Chicago: University of Chicago Press, 1987.

Tinto, V. "Stages of Student Departure: Reflections of the Longitudinal Character of Student Leaving." *Journal of Higher Education* 59(4): (1988).

Tinto, V. "Principles of Effective Retention." *Journal of the Freshman Year Experience* 2(1):35–48 (1990).

Todd, J., J. L. Mckinney, R. Harris, R. Chadderton, and L. Small. "Attitudes Toward Interracial Dating: Effects of Age, Sex, and Race." *Journal of Multicultural Counseling and Development* 20(4):202–208 (October 1992).

Torres, G. "Critical Race Theory: The Decline of the Universalist Ideal and the Hope of Plural Justice—Some Observations and Questions of an Emerging Phenomenon." *Minnesota Law Review* 75 (1991).

Treiman, J., and K. Terrell. "Sex and the Process of Status Attainment: A Comparison of Working Women and Men." *American Sociological Review* 40:174–200 (1975).

Trow, M. "Class, Race, and Higher Education in America." *American Behavioral Scientist* 35(4–5):585–605 (March-June 1992).

University of Arizona Factbook. Tucson: University of Arizona, Office of Institutional Research, 1993–94.

University of Arizona Record: 1993–94 General Catalog. Tucson: Arizona Board of Regents, April 1993.

Van Gennep, A. *The Rites of Passage,* translated by M. Vizedon and G. Caffee. Chicago: University of Chicago Press, 1960.

Villanueva, A. *La Llorona and Other Stories.* Tempe, Ariz.: Bilingual Press, 1994.

Weiler, K. *Women Teaching for Change: Gender, Class and Power.* South Hadley, Mass.: Bergin and Garvey, 1988.

Weis, L. *Issues in Education: Schooling and the Reproduction of Class and Gender Inequalities.* Occasional Paper No. 10. Buffalo: State University of New York, 1982.

Weis, L. *Between Two Worlds: Black Students in an Urban Community College.* Boston: Routledge and Kegan Paul, 1985.

Weis, L. *Race, Class and Schooling.* Amherst: State University of New York at Buffalo, Comparative Education Center, 1986.

Weis, L., and M. Fine. *Beyond Silenced Voices: Class, Race, and Gender in United States Schools.* SUNY Frontiers in Education Series. Albany: State University of New York Press, 1993.

West, C. "Brendan Brown Lecture: Reassessing the Critical Legal Studies Movement." *Loyola University Law Review* 34:265 (1988).

West, C. "The Role of Law in Progressive Politics." *Vanderbilt University Law Review* 43:1797 (1990).

West, C. *Race Matters.* New York: Vintage Books, 1993.

Wharfield, H. B. "Border Fight at Nogales." In *The Black Military Experience in the American West,* edited by J. M. Carroll, 505–511. New York: Liveright, 1971.

Widrick, S. "Is Higher Education a Negative Product?" *College Board Review* 130:27–29 (Winter 1983).

Wilcox, P. "Social Policy and White Racism." *Social Policy* 1 (1970).

Wiley, E., III. "Educator Stresses Role of Cultural Centers in Survival of Minorities at Predominantly White Campuses." *Black Issues in Higher Education* 5(21):18 (January 19, 1989).

Williams, P. J. *The Alchemy of Race and Rights: Diary of a Law Professor.* Cambridge, Mass.: Harvard University Press, 1991.

Willis, P. *Learning to Labor.* Farnborough, England: Saxon House, 1977.

Yess, J. P. "The Influence of Marriage on Community College Student Achievement in Specific Programs of Study." *Research in Higher Education* 14(2):103–118 (1991).

Yetman, N. R., ed. *Majority and Minority: The Dynamics of Race and Ethnicity in American Life.* Boston: Allyn and Bacon, 1991.

Zweigenhaft, R. L. *Blacks in the White Establishment? A Study of Race and Class in America.* New Haven, Conn.: Yale University Press, 1991.

Ivy Leaf Club, 59

Jews, 103
Johnson, Marvin D. "Swede," 128
Jolivet, Anna: clubs and organizations, 58, 59; college plans, counselors, 18; racism, emotions, 101; racism, orientation, 91; working, 74, 93, 94
Jolly Jensen Lassies, 58, 59
Jones, Lena, 48, 93, 102, 130, 131

Lander, Cressworth, 33, 89, 96, 101, 115, 136
Larriva, G. A., 34, 45, 52, 57–59, 62, 103
Latin Students of America, 57, 59
law firms, 111
law school, 108, 109, 111, 112
Lee, Olden, 19, 48, 69, 90, 99, 134
Lemon, Robin, 19, 66, 69
Lesher, John, 126
loneliness, 102
Lopez, Juanita, 43, 44
Los Universitarios, 60–62, 84, 85
LULAC, 130

Maddox, Lester, 118
Márquez, Alfredo, 32, 53, 65, 137, 138
marriage, 66–68, 75
Martínez, Evelia, 26, 65, 76, 85, 123, 130
Mathews, William, 64
Matsuda, Mari, 83, 84
McCray, Ernie: activism, 116, 117; friends, 68; Greek life, 54; parents, 47, 48; racism, 90, 95, 98, 99, 101
McKee, Mildred Hudson, ix, xii, 18, 47, 87, 100
MEChA, 70, 71, 120, 121, 123, 130
Mexican American Liberation Committee, 120
Mexican American Student Association, 120

Mexican Revolution, 41–43
military service, 32, 33
Miller, George, 65
Minority Action Council, 131
Mitchell, Eddie, 98

National Council of La Raza, 117
Navarrette, Diego, 49, 60, 68
Navarrette, Elena, 60, 67
New Start, 71, 122
Newman Center, 61, 119, 120
Nogales High School, 103
Nuñez, Ed, 32

organizations, 57–63, 115–130
organizing, 122
orientation, freshmen, 91, 93
Ott, Mary, 22, 45, 53, 84

parents, 12, 18–35, 41–48, 136–140
Pesqueira, Richard, 45, 46, 55, 56, 61, 84
Phrateres, 59
plans, college, 13, 17–19, 22–26, 29, 31, 33–35
Post, Anita, 58
Preciado, Hortense, 24
priests, 121
professors: African American, 95, 96; general, 86–90, 93, 108, 110, 125; supportive, 122
protests, 129
Pueblo High School, 32, 70, 71, 118, 121

racism: admissions officers, 121; classroom, ix, 87–90, 104, 105, 108; counselors, 19, 25–27, 30, 31, 35; dormitories, 91, 92; fraternities, xi; grades, 86, 87, 109; Greek system, 128; orientation, 91, 93; persistence of, 136; police, 99; professors, 86–90, 93, 106; restaurants, 101, 114; subtle, 102; swimming, ix, 93; violence, xi

< About the Author

Jay M. Rochlin is the grandson of Russian Jewish immigrants who settled in Nogales, Arizona, on the U.S. border with Mexico, where he grew up. He has a Ph.D. in higher education from the University of Arizona, and for the past thirteen years has been editor of the University of Arizona's alumni magazine. Prior to that he was in the television industry in various administrative and production capacities.